# LAWYER
## INTERRUPTED

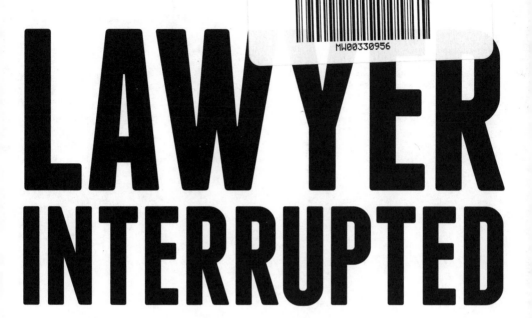

# LAWYER
## INTERRUPTED

Successfully Transitioning
from the Practice of Law—
and Back Again

# AMY IMPELLIZZERI

Cover design by Kelly Book/ABA Design.

Printed in the United States of America.

19 18 17 16 15 5 4 3 2 1

ISBN: 978-1-63425-222-5

e-ISBN: 978-1-63425-223-2

### Library of Congress Cataloging-in-Publication Data

Impellizzeri, Amy, author.
  Lawyer interrupted : successfully transitioning from the practice of law -- and back again / Amy Impellizzeri.
     pages cm
  ISBN 978-1-63425-222-5 (softcover : alk. paper) -- ISBN 978-1-63425-223-2 (e book) 1. Law--Vocational guidance--United States. 2. Career changes--United States. 3. Employment re-entry--United States. I. Title.
  KF297.I47 2015
  340.023'73--dc23                                                      2015012219

Discounts are available for books ordered in bulk. Special consideration is given to state bars, CLE programs, and other bar-related organizations. Inquire at Book Publishing, ABA Publishing, American Bar Association, 321 N. Clark Street, Chicago, Illinois 60654-7598.

www.ShopABA.org

To Paul, Paul, Luke, and Grace.
For the interruptions.
And the reasons.

# Contents

# Foreword

If I could, I would give every lawyer in the United States a copy of *Lawyer Interrupted*. My well-educated guess is that every lawyer either has wondered at some point whether she is on the right path or knows someone who has at least occasional doubts about her career trajectory. Amy Impellizzeri is a talented writer who knows from personal experience both how difficult and how rewarding a career change can be. In this book, she provides an immensely useful guide to all of the ways in which lawyers and law students can expand their range of what is possible with a law degree.

What *Lawyer Interrupted* does, more than any other book to date, is collect the best advice for all stages and types of career questioning that lawyers may have and to present it in an immensely enjoyable and highly readable way. Above all, it gives realistic advice for navigating a career break or transition. It provides sound strategies not only for professional exploration and development but also for the real-life, off-resume issues that so many lawyers have to struggle with as they move from one phase of their work life to the next.

Another important aspect of this book is its publisher. The imprimatur of the American Bar Association is perhaps the most significant sign that the legal profession itself is recognizing the adaptability of the JD. Just a few years ago, I would not have expected the ABA to welcome the idea of lawyers' career reinvention, let alone support a book that facilitates such reinventions so beautifully. My hope is that the ABA's recognition that lawyers benefit from creative thought at all stages of their career will lead to many fewer unhappy lawyers and, consequently, a much stronger legal profession.

When I was an unhappy lawyer, the senior lawyers around me talked about career change in much the same way I imagine people used to talk about cancer in the 1950s—in whispers, if at all. It seemed to me that leaving the law was a sign of failure, something to be ashamed of. And so, for many years, I made a series of patchwork but professionally acceptable changes in an effort to remedy my growing dissatisfaction. I changed firms twice within the same city and then changed coasts. These quietly desperate moves will be familiar to many unhappy lawyers and former lawyers and did not fix a thing.

If only I had had *Lawyer Interrupted* back then! As it was, when I left my law firm partnership, I spent years researching options and talking to former lawyers who had gone down more interesting and varied paths than I had ever imagined. My research turned into *Life After Law: Finding Work You Love with the J.D. You Have,* a practical guide to developing an alternative career. I wrote *Life After Law* in large part because guides like *Lawyer Interrupted* didn't exist then. I also wanted other unhappy lawyers to have easier access to the many, many role models for using your law degree and legal training in unusual ways.

My own story, like Amy's, illustrates the power of interrupting and reconsidering your career. After some false starts and wrong turns—I mean, experiments—I began my dream job as a business professor teaching law and ethics to undergraduates and MBA students. And while no job is perfect every day (*see,* e.g., grading papers, writing exams), I can truly say that I love what I do. Teaching and counseling students give me a sense of flow and purpose that I never felt in private practice. This is wonderful both for me and for my family. Not only do they get to see me more, they get to see me happy.

In the last few years, reconsidering one's law career has become less stigmatized and more socially acceptable. Personally, I'm thrilled by this development. Lawyers should be less concerned about stepping away from tradition and more open to the myriad possibilities of different ways to work. As more of them do so and talk about it and share the kind of best practices presented in *Lawyer Interrupted,* there will be ripple effects that benefit everyone. In my own research, I've found that many lawyers' career changes were sparked by meeting someone else who understood just how valuable and fungible their "legal" skills were. Over time, my hope is that lawyers will develop a broader and more realistic set of ideas about the variety of ways in which they can put their legal education to use.

Every lawyer should read this book, whether or not he or she is ready to make a change. In my experience, most lawyers have days, if not years, of wondering whether there is something more out there. It is entirely normal for attorneys to wonder whether they would be better off in another area of law and for law students to wonder whether they are on the right path. The stunning rates of clinical depression, alcoholism, and firm flight among lawyers suggests that perhaps many more lawyers should be asking themselves the same thing. Questioning the traditional law career paradigm is more common than most people—especially most nonlawyers—realize. These thoughts are not only normal but healthy. The unexamined career path is not worth following.

Even lawyers who love the law—and I am one of them—may not want to practice law for all of their working lives. Why should they? We don't expect business school graduates to stay in the same position throughout their careers. We should not expect this of lawyers either. The JD is at least as versatile as the MBA, and yet lawyers have not had the same broad cultural and professional support for career variation that business school graduates have had. That support is well deserved and long overdue.

The world needs more interrupted lawyers, reconsidered lawyers, and others like them. They, in turn, need this book. As I explained in *Life After Law*, law school and law practice hone a wide range of generally useful skills including analysis, problem-solving, communication, persuasion, project management, counseling, and advocating for change. Law school graduates usually enjoy using one or more of those skills, which can often be more enjoyable and, arguably, more valuable beyond the traditional practice of law. There is tremendous untapped potential in the dissatisfied lawyers who fill the ranks of firms and government offices, if they can only find a more satisfying and sustainable way to use those skills. *Lawyer Interrupted* is an invaluable resource for doing just that.

There is never a wrong time to reconsider the direction your legal career is taking. In speaking with unhappy lawyers across the country, I've met people who embarked on new and more fulfilling careers 30 or more years into their careers, when some of their colleagues were considering retirement. I've also spoken with dozens of law students who already know that traditional legal work is not for them and are not waiting until they burn out as a midlevel associate to follow what truly excites them. *Lawyer Interrupted* provides terrific advice for anyone who is reconsidering the path they are on, no matter how far down that path they are.

I couldn't be happier to introduce *Lawyer Interrupted*. It provides the essential tools you need to create a career you truly love. That is something everyone—no matter how smart, accomplished, young, old, or "successful"—deserves to have.

—Liz Brown

# About the Author

From the beginning, Amy Impellizzeri had one professional goal: to be a lawyer.

She graduated Dickinson College with a B.A. in both English and Philosophy (*cum laude*) in 1992, and then graduated with honors from George Washington National Law Center in 1995.

Amy served as law clerk to The Honorable Gary Golkiewicz, Chief Special Master of the Court of Federal Claims, from 1995 to 1997, where she aided him in adjudicating cases across the country brought pursuant to the National Childhood Vaccine Injury Act of 1986.

In 1997, Amy joined the civil litigation firm Landman Corsi Ballaine & Ford P.C., where her practice focused on jury trial work and appellate work in New Jersey and Pennsylvania, in areas including product liability, premises liability, E&O liability, FELA liability, and insurance coverage.

In January 2000, Amy joined the Mass Torts Department of Skadden Arps in New York City, where—for just under a decade—her focus was on developing and coordinating litigation strategy for public and national companies with pending multi-state lawsuits that included, *inter alia*, product liability, conspiracy, fraud, negligence, breach of contract, and bad faith allegations. Amy's trial-related work included specialization in expert witness issues, including recruitment and development of expert witnesses for clients, as well as research and preparation for depositions and cross-examinations of adversaries' expert witnesses.

While at Skadden Arps, Amy also represented New York City in examinations before trial as a Special Assistant Corporate Counsel, and regularly represented indigent families who were seeking appropriate placement and special education services pursuant to federal and state law for children classified as emotionally and/or learning disabled. Amy was profiled by the

New York Lawyers for Public Interest in the spring of 2006 for her *pro bono* work in this regard.

In June 2009, Amy left Skadden Arps to write and advocate for working women, consulting with groups including New York City's A Better Balance, and later joining the executive team of Hybrid Her, recognized in 2010 and 2011 by *ForbesWoman* as one of the "Top 100 Websites for Women."

Amy's first novel, *Lemongrass Hope*, debuted as an Amazon Best Seller (Fantasy/Romance and Fantasy/Time Travel) and has been acclaimed by book reviewers, bloggers, and authors alike. Oprah's very first Book Club Selection author and *New York Times* #1 bestselling author Jacquelyn Mitchard has said, "*Lemongrass Hope* is that fine and fresh thing—a truly new story. . . . Amy Impellizzeri is a bold and tender writer, who makes the impossible feel not only real, but strangely familiar." Another *New York Times* bestselling author, Caroline Leavitt, called *Lemongrass Hope* "haunting, mesmerizing and unforgettable." *Kirkus Reviews* hailed it as "a layered, bittersweet romance that questions consequences and explores second chances."

Amy's essays and articles have appeared in *The Huffington Post*, *The Glass Hammer*, *Divine Caroline*, and ABA's *Law Practice Today*, among others.

*Lawyer Interrupted* is Amy's nonfiction book debut.

# Introduction

On June 1, 2009, in the middle of the most tumultuous economic period I had experienced in my professional life, I did something that many might consider very strange.

I voluntarily left a very good, very lucrative, very coveted . . . job.

Actually, I left my career. As a corporate litigator.

For more than 13 years, I had been immersed in depositions, trials, motions *in limine*, and summary judgment arguments. I tried my first case before I was 30 and went on to work for one of the most prestigious litigation departments in one of the most respected law firms in the country.

Frankly, before starting my litigation career, I had never wanted to be anything other than a litigator, and once I started practicing I barely had time to think about anything other than practicing law. But when my firm, Skadden Arps, announced its "Sidebar Plus" program in the spring of 2009, I, like many others at the firm, was surprised and intrigued. For the first time, I found myself seriously entertaining whether there might be an entirely new professional path waiting for me on the other side.

The Sidebar Plus policy was essentially Skadden Arps's alternative to the massive layoffs other firms were employing at the commencement of the economic storm signaled by the 2008 Lehman Brothers collapse. Under Sidebar Plus, any attorney could apply for a year-long leave of absence to do something productive outside of the firm: do volunteer work, start a new business, or travel to Australia. If the application was granted, the Sidebar Plus participant would receive one-third of her or his salary as a stipend for the year and could return to the previous position with the firm in one year's time.

Interestingly enough, the policy seemed to be premised on the idea that many of the transactional and mergers & acquisitions attorneys who had found their inbox piles diminishing due to the economic crunch would jump at a chance for a year off. In reality, many of the applicants were litigators—like me—whose inboxes are largely impervious to economic meltdowns. In fact, when I applied for Sidebar Plus, the head of my department sighed, "But you're so busy! Why would you want to leave?"

"It's just a year," I said.

*Just a year.*

I lined up advocacy and *pro bono* work even before I turned out the lights of my 42nd-floor office in Times Square. I applied for and was accepted to write a new online column for working mothers and started making a list of things I would do for the year.

And not do.

For example, I did not return phone calls of people I didn't want to talk to. I did not finish books if they didn't grab me right away. I did not finish meals that weren't delicious. It was, in fact, my year of doing only what I wanted to do.

By the end of that year, I had done something I had never expected: I had successfully and happily transitioned from the practice of law.

*Just a year.*

Significantly, I had no gap in my résumé. Most importantly, I had no regrets. No regrets about transitioning, and no regrets about the 13 years of experience as a corporate litigator. Not one.

I am convinced that a successful transition from the practice of law—for lawyers who want to do so—need not create a void or a gap, either literally or figuratively. Right from the start of my own one-year sabbatical, I set out to ensure that my time away from the law was meaningful and productive. At the start of my participation in Skadden's Sidebar Plus, I did not, I admit, have a clear idea of what the first year would look like. I certainly had no idea at that time what the years after would look like. And even though I blew through that stipend pretty quickly and made no meaningful salary for the next year (and somewhat beyond), I credit my Sidebar Plus year as being an invaluable investment in my professional journey, one that ultimately resulted in real returns—both intangible and financial.

In the summer of 2013, I was contacted by an agent, Kathy Welton, who said that she had read my piece in the *ABA's Law Practice Today* about my experience in Sidebar Plus. She told me that she really wanted to pitch a book to the ABA about successfully transitioning from the practice of law and that she wanted me to be the one to write the book. I responded simply: "You have just described the book I have been wanting to write for four years now."

And so it began. The ABA accepted our proposal less than two months after submission, and *Lawyer Interrupted* was born.

This book synthesizes research, advice from experts in the areas of career counseling and recruitment, and interviews with formerly and currently practicing attorneys who are doing some amazing things and who have inspirational stories to tell about their journeys.

I truly believe that this book is a must-read resource for all attorneys and law students who find themselves—at some point—evaluating their decisions to practice law.

It is not a book for attorneys who have not thought for even one moment about leaving the practice of law. But I suspect that if you're still with me here . . . that's not you.

# Chapter 1

# A Preflight Checklist

## How to Avoid Pitfalls and Disasters

## Before You Even Take a Break

*Listen. It's a process. Right? I tell people who ask me—if you really want to follow your passion of making clay pots, that's great. Good for you. But you better take a pottery class, first. You know what I mean? You better plan for it.*

—Nathan Sawaya, internationally famous lawyer-turned-artist

In 2009, I was covering a New York area iRelaunch conference for a local column I was writing at the time. I was just about to commence a one-year sabbatical from corporate law, and I had been invited to the conference as a media guest.

iRelaunch, originally co-founded by Carol Fishman Cohen and Vivian Steir Rabin, also co-authors of *Back on the Career Track* (Hachette Book Group USA, 2007), is an internationally renowned company that helps former professionals re-enter the workforce after a hiatus. The conference was full of practical advice for would-be relaunchers, and powered by infectious enthusiasm. But one thought nagged at me as I sat in on a session called "Fixing the Gap," on relaunching résumés, and listened to concerns and regrets from relaunchers: *Wouldn't it be great if everyone thought about the gap at the beginning of their hiatus? Wouldn't it be great,* I remember thinking, *if you could somehow prevent the gap, rather than work so hard to fix it later on?*

In other words, for the seasoned attorney who has carefully molded and shaped his or her career path, shouldn't the hiatus or transition from practicing law be just as well thought out—just as planned—as every professional step before it? Conversely, for those lawyers, like Nathan Sawaya, internationally famous Lego brick artist, who concedes that his legal career was one that he fell into on his way to doing something else, shouldn't the hiatus or transition from practicing law be the *first* planned-out step on your résumé?

The simple truth is that you can prevent or mitigate literal and figurative gaps on your résumé, even if you are indeed taking a break from the practice of law. I have clocked in hundreds of hours interviewing former and current lawyers. I have talked to experts in the fields of legal training, ethics, career counseling, and career recruiting. Although there are certainly variations in specific pieces of advice for those wishing to leave or take a break from the practice of law, certain commonalities emerge that are worth talking about here.

*At the beginning.*

1. Be sure you really want to leave
2. Leave on top
3. Cultivate relationships with junior colleagues
4. Keep dressing like a lawyer
5. Engage in a pattern of strategic volunteerism
6. Embrace it!

## Be Sure You Really Want to Leave

While many parents would still like their children to grow up to become doctors or lawyers, surveys also show that up to half of all practicing lawyers would not actually recommend the profession to their own children.[1]

After Samuel Bellicini, currently of Fishkin Slatter, LLP, resigned from the practice of law with charges pending in 1994, he fought hard to overcome addiction and gambling problems that had interfered with and interrupted the professional aspirations he had harbored since he was a teen. "You have to understand, I had wanted to be an attorney since I was 16 years old." About his hard-fought reinstatement to the practice of law in 2009, he says: "I still feel there is no more important or prestigious professional license in the history of Western civilization than being a member of the Bar of the great State of California. And you can quote me on that."

Nevertheless, when I asked him about his own teen son—"So how would you feel about your son becoming a lawyer? Like you?"—he paused and then finally conceded that he wouldn't necessarily want that life for his son.

With good reason.

There is some convincing evidence that lawyers beat out many other professionals in terms of rates of depression, substance abuse, and alcoholism.[2] In fact, according to data from the Centers for Disease Control (CDC), lawyers rank fourth highest in number of suicides, behind pharmacists, physicians, and dentists. Lawyers are 3.6 times more likely to suffer depression than nonlawyers.[3] By some reports, about 20 percent of lawyers suffer from clinical depression—twice the national average.[4]

These frightening statistics are beginning to get people to stand up and take notice. The state of Kentucky, for example, is so concerned about its lawyers that it has begun leading its annual CLE conference with a presentation on suicide awareness. Yvette Hourigan, who runs the Kentucky Lawyer Assistance Program, points out: "There are a lot of high stress professions. . . . Being a physician has stress. However[,] when the surgeon goes into the surgical suite to perform his surgery, they don't send another physician in to try to kill the patient. You know, they're all on the same team trying to do one job. In the legal profession, adversity is the name of the game."[5]

It is clear, of course, that the adversarial pressures do not suddenly arise for the first time when lawyers begin practicing law out in the world. In fact, they seem to begin as early as law school. One study found that 40 percent of law students suffered from depression by the time they graduated.[6] Many law students are reluctant to report developing mental issues, because "most state bars make subjective decisions as to whether mental illness or depression, treated or untreated, are barriers to a candidate's certification to practice law."[7]

"Does law school just naturally attract depressed or sad people?" I asked attorney Susan Cartier Liebel. This was in 2014, when we were discussing her venture, Solo Practice University, which helps many discontented lawyers restart their professional lives in a new direction. "Not at all," Susan said emphatically. "I think it's just the opposite. Law school attracts incredibly creative, dynamic personalities."

*So, what happens next?*

Perhaps, in the case of many law students at least, the root of the problem can be traced back even prior to admission to law school. Law school is, for many, still an avenue pursued by college grads bowing to societal and familial pressures, even though they themselves are unsure about their long-term desire to practice law. *Life After Law* author Liz Brown points out: "Law is still a generally respected profession, lawyer jokes notwithstanding."[8]

Lawyer-turned-professional-artist Nathan Sawaya concurs: "My parents were always really supportive of my art. But I didn't have faith in my art as a viable profession. There were some societal pressures working there." So, following his undergraduate career at New York University, Sawaya says he made the "logical choice for an aspiring artist graduating from NYU." He went to law school . . . and then found himself among the ranks of those dissatisfied with the choice.

The dissatisfaction described by Sawaya and others is not universal, of course, but it is pervasive. Brown points out, "Law may be the only profession with a sub-profession dedicated to helping people get out of it."[9]

Of course, the discontent among practicing lawyers does not stem from lack of money or prestige. A 2014 study found some evidence that today's law students actually come from the wealthiest American families, and hope to top their parents' salaries.[10] But are high salaries really *all* these aspiring lawyers want? There is also convincing evidence that law students would prefer to trade long hours and the so-called "perks" offered by top firms that are designed to keep associates at the office—such as car services and expensed dinners—for lower salaries. A report by the legal advocacy group A Better Balance, entitled "Seeking a Just Balance," was compiled from a survey of New York University law students. According to the report, 70 percent of respondents, including men and women, expected to make career sacrifices in order to have a satisfying personal life.[11] They did not, it seems, expect that career success and personal success were *both* achievable.

With all of this dissatisfaction, stress, and depression, it is no wonder that more than half of lawyers leave private firm practice by their fifth year.[12] But, as Marc Luber, founder of the award-winning video website JDCareersOutThere.com, points out, some of this exodus population may really be seeking a new career practicing different law.

Luber, a former successful legal recruiter who started his career as an entertainment lawyer, founded JDCareersOutThere.com in 2013 to fill the void created by law schools that arguably do a poor job of educating students about the plethora of available legal careers "out there." Through this online membership forum that acts as a substitute for time-intensive informational interviewing, Luber has created a resource through which lawyers who might just be in the wrong place can investigate other fields. In 2014, for example, Luber interviewed prominent members of growing areas of law, including tax law, trusts and estates, elder law (not to be confused with estate planning; elder law focuses on how to help the living), intellectual property, bankruptcy, and foreclosure.[13]

In addition to investigating whether you are in the wrong field of law altogether, before exiting the legal field, you might just want to consider whether the reason you want to leave is because—quite simply—you are working too hard. As iRelaunch's Carol Cohen points out, many dissatisfied lawyers run from the law without thinking about the options still available within the purview of a legal career. Cohen advises that you first ask yourself some important questions: Have you explored the possibility of a flex arrangement? Is a non-equity partnership track available to you? How about a part-time position?

And if you are going to dismiss the possibility of flex time or part-time work as one reserved only for women—or only for caregivers—let me stop you *right there.*

Flex work and reduced scheduling are *not* gender-specific issues. As some very compelling recent research has indicated, we are—all of us—suffering from a culture of overwork.[14] Compartmentalizing flex work as an alternative reserved only for women, or only for caregivers, does a broad disservice to professionals, including lawyers, who are trapped in an arguably and pervasively flawed professional structure. In a paper presented at the "Gender and Work: Challenging Conventional Wisdom" Research Symposium held by the Harvard Business School in March of 2013, researchers Irene Padavic (Florida State University) and Robin J. Ely (Harvard University) argued that many organizations "rely on the work-family narrative as an explanation for women's blocked mobility partly because it diverts attention from the broader problem of a long-hours work culture among professionals."

> The readily-available work-family narrative allows firms and their members to avoid this reality and the anxieties it creates by projecting the problem exclusively onto women and by projecting the image of a successful employee exclusively onto men. Ironically, this focus leads to accommodation policies (such as moving to part time) that do little to help women and often hurt them. Meanwhile, the larger problem remains unaddressed and unacknowledged, penalizing all employees and limiting firms' ability to accomplish their primary tasks . . . .
>
> Although virtually all participants pointed to work-family conflict as the reason women quit or failed to make partner, our analysis showed women felt no greater distress than men over long work hours and over work-family conflict. Both sexes were equally (and highly) dissatisfied on these dimensions, revealing a disconnect between the facts and the firm's problem-definition. The second disconnect was the fact that a key "presenting problem," to use psychological language, was the differential turnover rate, when in fact, there was no difference: Company records indicate that women and men had quit at the same rate for at least the preceding three years. The third and final disconnect was firm leaders' negative reaction to the analyses and proposed interventions. They had requested an analysis of the firm's organizational culture; yet upon hearing that the gender problem was only a piece of a larger work-management problem and that the solution would involve a change in work practices that transcended work-family accommodations, they rejected the analysis on grounds that it did not focus explicitly on women. Leaders' apparent wish to retain their original assessment—that gender was the firm's primary

HR problem, that the nature of the gender problem was women's difficulty balancing work and family, and that men were largely immune to such difficulties—required a rejection of evidence on the part of evidence-driven analysts, which we found notable.[15]

Law firms are not immune to organizational culture analysis. In fact, thanks largely to the championing of advocates such as Deborah Epstein Henry and others, the structure of law firms has been analyzed from the inside out in recent years, and options such as flex time, part time, and telecommuting that were not available even a decade ago are now on the table. Consider these prior to exiting the practice of law altogether.[16]

Of course, once you have examined and explored other available options in the legal field, or alternative legal careers, or flex-time options, and have decided that you still want to take a break from practicing law, there are effective steps to take at the very beginning of your break that are more likely to make the break a positive and productive time in your career path. The remainder of this chapter outlines these important moves.

## Leave on Top

Once you are convinced that you truly want to leave your law firm position entirely, whether for another career in the law (see Chapter 5) or to be a full-time caregiver (Chapter 3) or for another reason altogether (Chapter 6), you will still want to plan your exit carefully and thoughtfully from the start.

If you can.

If you are leaving involuntarily, this piece of advice may not necessarily work for you. Have no fear. Chapter 4 is your resource for practically and successfully transitioning to an involuntary hiatus, complete with interviews and advice from peers who have been in your shoes.

For those leaving the practice of law voluntarily, the most important and universal piece of advice gleaned from interviewing professionals in legal and professional recruitment is to try as best you can to leave at a time when you are close to the top of your professional career to date. As iRelaunch's Carol Cohen points out, "You will be 'frozen in time' when you leave." Do not,

Cohen emphatically recommends, wait until chaos or conflict in your personal life compromises your work performance. Do not wait until you are forced out. Leave at the height of your current performance level (or as close to it as possible), and recognize that your potential will not be lost. "High-potential women and men don't lose their potential just because they step away from their careers for a few moments," says Cohen. She should know: Carol Cohen is a mother of four who took 11 years out of the full-time workforce before her return to investment firm Bain Capital (which was documented in a Harvard Business School case study about professional career re-entry).[17]

Cohen's advice bears out in real-world examples. Take Jill Donovan, who left her law firm more than a decade ago to be a caregiver to her first child. She left such a positive impression on her colleagues and superiors that a few years later, when former colleague and former Oklahoma state court judge Todd Singer needed a co-adjunct professor to teach trial practice, he called upon Donovan to join him, even though she had not actually engaged in trial practice (or any legal practice) in several years. (Later Jill Donovan went on to become a renowned jewelry designer, a fascinating path we will explore in more detail in Chapter 6.) Judge Singer says that he just knew Donovan would do a great job, because of his experience working with her at their prior firm. It did not matter to him one iota that she had been out of the practice of law for several years, as a full-time caregiver to her young children.

Past ABA President Laurel Bellows, who herself took a one-year sabbatical from law firm practice to carry out her duties as ABA president from 2012 to 2013, provides another telling anecdote. I asked Bellows about her own experience, as managing partner of The Bellows Law Group, with interviewing and hiring attorneys who had "breaks" on their résumés, and she shared her insight: "Yes, I have hired an attorney with a nine-year child-raising break. She was a trained litigator and a self-starter who maintained strong relationships with clients, communicated frequently, was very cautious to research the law to assure she was up-to-date, and was willing to ask questions when in doubt, eliminating the risk of guesswork."

The experts agree that every transitioning attorney has tremendous potential down the road, and attorneys who "leave on top" and stay connected to the profession may very well realize that tremendous potential with the most ease.

## Cultivate Relationships with Junior Colleagues

In 1999, I represented a large client that was involved in thousands of lawsuits claiming occupational diseases. We litigated the cases aggressively. The legal issues were as hotly contested as the factual issues, and the plaintiffs' first expert witness was excluded after lengthy briefings based on *Daubert v. Merrell Dow Pharmaceuticals*, 509 U.S. 579 (1993), a decision that was still considered to be in its infancy at the time. When the plaintiffs retained a new expert, Dr. L, I—along with numerous other co-counsel from other firms—was sent to help depose him, as I had worked personally on the *Daubert* briefing for my firm, and knew the legal issues inside and out. I can remember that deposition room as if it was yesterday . . . filled with dark suits and serious expressions.

The deposition went on for hours, and I hadn't even had a chance to ask a single question before everyone realized it was dark outside and they were all parked in nearby garages that were about to close. I had taken a train to the deposition, so I had no such concerns. Dr. L had been driven to the deposition, so he had no concerns either. We all decided to keep going with the deposition—late into the night—but everyone took a break and left to move their cars first.

Everyone except Dr. L and me, that is. Even the court reporter left. Even the attorneys who had driven Dr. L to the deposition left. I buried my head in my notes and outline, and Dr. L went to use the restroom. When he came back into the room, I ignored him. He didn't like that.

He started humming and dancing, trying to get my attention.

*A jig,* I thought. *He's dancing a jig.* I glanced up at him briefly. He was airborne for a moment, feet clicking up to one side.

Truly.

And he said gleefully, "I really don't care how long this takes. I hope it takes all night. After all, I'm getting paid by the hour."

I put my head back in my notes and resumed ignoring him. He continued dancing and clucking, right up until the other attorneys started streaming back in.

Near the end of the deposition, I finally got my turn to question Dr. L. As the lone woman in the room, and the youngest in the room, I was used to taking my turn toward the end. I started my questioning with: "Dr. L, how much are you charging today—per hour—for your testimony in these cases?"

"She's an attorney?" Dr. L turned to the attorney to his right, who nodded and told the surprised and now-embarrassed doctor that he was going to have to answer all of my questions. Dr. L had dismissed the junior attorney in the room too lightly—a big mistake.

Don't you make the same one.

In addition to leaving your firm on top, it is important to be thoughtful about maintaining relationships with former colleagues while on a break. While many attorneys keep in touch with their superiors, iRelaunch's Carol Cohen advises attorneys (and other professionals as well) not to ignore the need to cultivate relationships with junior colleagues.[18] "They are the ones who will continue on and advance while you are gone. Thus, they just might be the ones opening doors later on," Cohen points out.

So keep that standing lunch date with colleagues you yourself have mentored during your time practicing law. Keep your LinkedIn account active and updated. Make sure to connect with juniors and peers in the virtual world now so that you can follow their career paths after you leave. Keep up to date with junior colleagues' relevant movements up the ladder and be sure to send genuine and personal congratulatory messages as you learn of their accomplishments and promotions.

In sum, on your way out and as you embark on your professional break, it is important to leave a favorable impression, not just on the established stars such as the Judge Singers of your firm, but also on the rising stars at the firm.

No taking them lightly.

And whatever you do—no jigs.

## Keep Dressing Like a Lawyer

When you leave the practice of law, it is tempting to start crossing off things you think you will not need any more, at least for the short term. Things like courtroom suits, hefty dry-cleaning bills, bar memberships, CLE credits, and your subscription to legal journals start looking like burdensome expenses you no longer need.

Not. So. Fast.

As career coaches, including iRelaunch's Carol Cohen, advise: Do not cancel your newspaper subscription (or better yet—get one! You might actually have a little time to read it now). Do not cancel bar memberships. Do not stop taking CLE classes. In short, get dressed up and pretend you are a lawyer each morning, or at least until you have another gig lined up.

While writing this book, I interviewed many attorneys who relaunched their legal careers after 3-. 7-, 10-, and even 25-year breaks from the legal profession (see Chapter 10). Without exception, the ones who had kept their licenses and CLE credits active and up to date—like Susan Taylorson, currently an associate practicing real estate law at Gerstein Strauss & Rinaldi LLP, after a 25-year hiatus; and Camille Raia, currently general counsel of Platinum Health Care, after a decade-long hiatus—found that those current licenses and CLE credits made relaunching a much smoother experience than it might have been otherwise.

But what if, as you start to leave your legal career behind, you are absolutely, positively, totally certain that you do not want another legal career?

Ever?

*You need to at least entertain the possibility that you might, at some time in the future.*

For example, according to the results of a study by the Center for Work-Life Policy (now known as the Center for Talent of Innovation) of high-achieving professionals who voluntarily left the workforce between 2004 and 2009, after career breaks averaging 2½ years, 89 percent wanted to return to work.[19] It should be noted that this study population consisted of women who largely left for child-care reasons. Still, the success of organizations like iRelaunch (nearly one quarter of whose 2013 conference demographic was relaunching lawyers), the New Directions for Attorneys program at Pace Law School for relaunching lawyers, and Washington College of Law's Lawyer Re-Entry Program certainly supports the argument that any break from the practice of law should be presumed temporary unless and until proven otherwise.

Many relaunching attorneys I spoke with said they did not really think about going back until their personal circumstances changed: children started school full-time, children started college, or marriages broke up. As one relauncher told me poignantly, "No one really *expects* that their husband will have an affair and leave, but statistics show that half of all marriages end in divorce, and then what?"

In fact, experts and graduates from the ground-breaking New Directions for Attorneys at Pace Law School and other relaunching programs (see more discussion in Chapter 10) point to factors such as "dressing like a lawyer" during the break as potentially separating the successful relaunchers of the world from the unsuccessful. One simple rationale proffered for this distinction is that when and if you decide later on to head back into the practice of law or another profession altogether, you will need to show potential employers that you are indeed ready to engage. Experts and relaunching attorneys agree that potential employers are not likely to dwell on *why* you left. Given the statistics, your story will not be so unusual in that regard. But they *will* want to hear about what you did during your time away from the law. Perhaps more importantly, they will want to hear what you have done and are doing to ready yourself to re-enter the workforce. Put simply, they *will* want to hear commitment from you. Staying relatively up to date on professional licenses and CLE requirements, as well as current developments in your profession, will help make the case to prove your engagement and commitment.

Amy Gewirtz, Director of the New Directions for Attorneys program at Pace Law School, says that "dressing like a lawyer" should include continuous self-assessment; keeping skills fresh through advocacy work, pro bono work, and possible coursework; CLE updates; keeping a robust LinkedIn profile; maintaining a business card; and joining alumni groups. All of these recommendations are meant to serve one purpose: to keep your foot in the door of the legal profession.

Just in case.

## Engage in a Pattern of Strategic Volunteerism

Once you make that beeline away from your legal practice, even if your goal is to take time to do absolutely nothing—do *something*.

But make it a worthwhile something.

Justice Sandra Day O'Connor said that during her hiatus from the law to raise her two sons (from 1960 to 1965), she wanted to make sure to keep to her skills sharp and keep one foot in the field in some way. So, when she took on volunteer work, it was writing and grading exams for the Arizona bar. She also focused on political activity that ultimately created a network that helped her trajectory to the Supreme Court.[20]

In other words, alongside traveling, hiking, and making good on your dormant gym membership, maximize your time away from the law by lining up a few seminars and doing some community service. Above all, log a few meaningful hours of what Carol Cohen has called "strategic volunteering."

Marc Luber, founder of the award-winning video website JDCareersOutThere.com, says that advice he received at the beginning of his career from Bill Graham (producer of the legendary 1985 American Live Aid Concert) to "do lots of internships" was the most valuable advice he ever received. And took. In fact, Luber's humble willingness to intern at a low level at Bill Graham's company, after he graduated from law school, led to a dream opportunity of going out on tour with the Rolling Stones (think *Almost Famous!*). The Rolling Stones tour ultimately opened the door for Luber's successful career in the music industry, including managing bands, which in turn acted as a stepping stone to the eventual founding of his video website company, which serves as a virtual informational interviewing source for both law students and practicing lawyers.

Whether you call it "interning" or "strategic volunteering," the goal is the same. Offer to work for free in an environment where you can learn a new skill or learn something about a field in which you have never worked. You will likely find it quite easy to insinuate yourself into a new field, as people are generally pretty happy to secure free help from a lawyer. That is not to say that you should be practicing law for free, or at all, in your "break" time. (See more discussion of ethical issues in Chapter 9.) But you

how the "gap" will look on your résumé, in determin-
tely be filled.

...p or volunteer position might tell you a thing or two about
...ld you do not want to work in at all. Conversely, it might actually lead
to a career opportunity, if you should want one down the road. In their
book and on their website, *Back on the Career Track* co-authors Carol Fishman Cohen and Vivian Steir Rabin cite several examples of lawyers who
volunteered for nonprofit and other companies, only to be asked to work
for those companies eventually because employers saw up close the assets
and work ethic of the would-be relaunching attorneys.[21]

Indeed, a rather dramatic example of the success of strategic volunteerism
is the New Directions for Attorneys program, which includes a 3-month
externship for its participants, some of whom have been away from practice
for up to 30 years (or who have little or no legal experience). Although the
attorneys are not guaranteed job offers after the externships, many graduates tell stories of relaunching their careers based on the expertise and
confidence they learned during those "strategic volunteering" opportunities.

For example, Susan Taylorson, currently an associate at Gerstein Strauss
& Rinaldi LLP, leveraged an externship with the New York Attorney General's office, working in the real estate regulation department, into a second
career practicing real estate law.

Camille Raia, currently general counsel of Platinum Health Care, merged
re-entry with her desire to enter what she perceived as the booming area
of health care law, tenaciously seeking out an unpaid position with Hackensack Medical Center in New Jersey that later led to her current position.

Emilia Naccarato Roll, formerly assistant director of Career Services,
Employer Outreach, at Cardozo Law School, agrees that transitioning attorneys should try to find opportunities to keep their legal skills up to date,
even when performing volunteer hours in the most common setting of
all—your kids' schools. Roll suggests that if you are going to help out at
the kids' schools, seek out opportunities to get involved in financial decisions and curriculum-driven initiatives. "Don't just do the cupcake thing,"
Roll advises wisely. "Even if you think you'll never go back. Statistics show
that you just might."

Does this mean you cannot do any volunteering for volunteering's sake? Of course not—but if you incorporate strategic volunteer work right from the beginning of your hiatus, you can learn some valuable information about alternate careers down the road, while at the same time essentially eliminating any résumé gap before it even begins.

## Embrace It!

This final bit of advice applies regardless of whether your break is voluntary or involuntary. Whether you leave consciously and deliberately after lining up a new secure, steady job, or whether you leave running out the door without a single professional plan in place, you must remember to *embrace the break as a gift.* The career and recruiting experts agree that once you take a break and gain a little breathing space and perspective, you will be able to see all of the other options outside of law firm life, and certainly outside of big law firm life. And since this is clearly true, use the time—embrace the time.

Beth A. Biedronski, an attorney I spoke to in 2014, described for me how she took three years off from 2008 to 2011 to be a full-time caregiver to her two sons, before resuming the practice of law in 2011. Anxious about her decision to return to a law firm upon relaunching her career, Biedronski said she wished she had explored more options before jumping back into the law firm life. She expressed that she wished she had used the time for more than volunteer work at her sons' schools and heading up the preschool equivalent of the PTA. She expressed a love for DIY rehab projects, and regretted that she did not explore more opportunities to use that passion and skill during her hiatus, and explore ways to potentially monetize those skills. Perhaps most poignantly, Biedronski talked about how she wished that she had *enjoyed* the time off. "I didn't feel happy all the time, but in hindsight, I enjoyed about 60 to 75 percent of what I was doing. And you know what? That's actually a lot."

Marc Luber, founder of JDCareersOutThere.com, concurs, noting that many lawyers take a traditional route without being exposed to or knowing how many other routes there are. He has created an entire business dedicated to educating lawyers about alternative careers—realizing that for many, time away is a luxury that they unfortunately cannot afford. Luber recalls that his own one-year sabbatical as a caregiver for his cancer-stricken mother provided the perspective he ultimately needed to launch his innovative business, recognized as a Top Career Blog by an ABA Readers Poll in 2013.

As a good friend once told me when I headed back to my law firm career in 2004, after my first maternity leave, "You are so lucky. You have a chance now to miss your child." The same is true for the law. You may never have a chance to miss or appreciate what you never actually leave.

## Notes

1. *Why I Love Being a Lawyer*, A.B.A. J. (February 1, 2011), http://www .abajournal.com/magazine/article/why_i_love_being_a_lawyer.

2. Martin Seligman, *Authentic Happiness: Using the New Positive Psychology to Realize Your Potential for Lasting Fulfillment* (New York: Free Press, 2002), at 177.

3. Rosa Flores & Rose Marie Arce, *Why Are Lawyers Killing Themselves?*, CNN. com, (January 19, 2014), http://www.cnn.com/2014/01/19/us/lawyer-suicides.

4. Liz Brown, J.D., *Life After Law* (Massachusetts: Bibliomotion, 2013), at 1.

5. Rosa Flores & Rose Marie Arce, *Why Are Lawyers Killing Themselves?*, CNN. com, (January 19, 2014), http://www.cnn.com/2014/01/19/us/lawyer-suicides.

6. *Id.*

7. *Id.*

8. Liz Brown, J.D., *Life After Law* (Massachusetts: Bibliomotion, 2013), at 15.

9. *Id.* at 1.

10. *Who Had Richer Parents, Doctors or Artists?*" NPR.org (March 18, 2014) (citing The NLSY79, published by the Bureau of Labor Statistics), http://www.npr .org/blogs/money/2014/03/18/289013884/who-had-richer-parents-doctors-or-artists.

11. Nancy Rankin, Phoebe Taubman, & Yolanda Wu, *Seeking a Just Balance: Law Students Weigh in on Work and Family* (June 2008), http://www.abetterbalance .org/web/images/stories/Documents/general/reports/seekingajustbalance3.pdf.

12. Marlisse Silver Sweeney, *The Female Lawyer Exodus*, The Daily Beast (July 31, 2013), http://www.thedailybeast.com/witw/articles/2013/07/31/

the-exodus-of-female-lawyers.html (citing National Association for Legal Professionals).

13. http://jdcareersoutthere.com.

14. Robin J. Ely & Irene Padavic, *Work-Family Conflict Is Not the Problem. Overwork Is.*, Huffington Post (November 6, 2013), http://www.huffingtonpost.com/robin-j-ely/workfamily-conflict-is-no_b_4221360.html.

15. Robin J. Ely & Irene Padavic, *The Work-Family Narrative as a Social Defense*, http://www.hbs.edu/faculty/Publication%20Files/The%20Work-Family%20Narrative%20as%20a%20Social%20Defense_7f295d01-c861-4b3b-9534-747def995458.pdf, at 1-3.

16. Deborah Henry Epstein, *Law & Reorder: Legal Industry Solutions for Restructure, Retention, Promotion & Work/Life Balance* (ABA, 2010).

17. http://www.irelaunch.com/founders.

18. Carol Cohen & Vivian Rabin, *Back on the Career Track: A Guide for Stay-At-Home-Moms Who Want to Return to Work* (Hachette Book Group USA, 2007), at 112.

19. Jennifer Preston, *Helping Women Get Back in the Game*, N.Y. Times (March 17, 2014).

20. Carol Cohen & Vivian Rabin, *Back on the Career Track: A Guide for Stay-At-Home-Moms Who Want to Return to Work* (Hachette Book Group USA, 2007), at 178-79.

21. *Id.* at 113; see also www.irelaunch.com.

Chapter 2

# It's Only Temporary
## Taking a Leave of Absence

*Yes, I'd like to visit the moon, but I don't think I'd like to live there.*
*—"I Don't Want to Live on the Moon" by Jeff Moss*

Every night in downtown Austin, Texas, 1.5 million bats leave their roost under the Congress Avenue Bridge at dusk and set off to eat tens of thousands of pounds of insects before returning to their habitat—the underside of a city bridge.[1] I had the pleasure of watching the temporary migration first-hand in the spring of 2013.

These bats—Mexican free-tailed bats—in addition to being the official flying mammals of Texas (you have to love a state with its own flying mammal!), are actually part of a vulnerable species. This means that they are not endangered, but still in danger. Why? Well, apparently, their insistence upon staying together in large populations in only a few locales makes them vulnerable to habitat destruction.

Which sounds ominous.

And familiar.

You could argue that big law firm attorneys have much in common with Mexican free-tailed bats—and much to learn from them.

When I stood at that bridge at dusk one night in April 2013, studying the Austin skyline and watching the bats leave their bridge roost, I understood at once both why the bats live there and also why they leave.

Sometimes a temporary sojourn is exactly what is necessary to escape a vulnerable habitat. You may not want to stop being a Mexican free-tailed bat altogether. But you can leave the bridge and eventually go back.

How long can you be gone? And what should you do while you are gone? I'm glad you asked.

1. What a difference a year makes
2. Make friends with the younger kids on the playground
3. Keep active in the interim
4. The rules do not apply to you (for one year at least)
5. Keep testing the waters

## What a Difference a Year Makes

I offer this response repeatedly to the question "How long is too long?" Because, while there are rarely absolutes in the law, this one is pretty close. In fact, "What a difference a year makes" is the undisputed, unambiguous answer to the real question: How long can I take a temporary leave of absence without truly jeopardizing my legal career?

Still too cryptic?

Well, here's the thing. Every year you take off will show up on your résumé. Except the first one. So, if you take anything up to a year off, your résumé gap will be miniscule. Hardly noticeable. You were at Lawyer, More Lawyers, and Most Lawyers from 2000 to 2010? And then worked at Lawyers Are Us from 2011 to Present? Great. Non-issue.

If you take one year off, a few things will change, but not many.

For every year you take off after the first, the gap on your résumé widens and the eyebrows of future employers *may* go up proportionately to the number of years you mark in your "temporary" leave of absence.

Will one year hinder your chances of rejoining your prior firm, or joining a new one at year's end? Probably not.

One year into my own initial sabbatical, I was still getting job offers from new law firms, invitations from my prior firm to rejoin, and lunch invitations from hiring partners at local firms. While I would recommend that you accept those lunch offers, politely accept or decline the new offers, and make sure to keep the door open at your prior employer before you even take your sabbatical, my own experience—as confirmed anecdotally with the dozens of relaunching lawyers I interviewed for this book—certainly indicates that one year is rarely too long.

Carol Cohen, co-founder of iRelaunch, agrees with me. Cohen shares a validating anecdote about a lawyer who took a sabbatical from his law firm for just over a year to work as issues director for a presidential campaign, and who did not lose a single client upon his return. (The lawyer in question just so happened to be Cohen's husband!)

Kim Yonta, former assistant prosecutor in New Jersey for more than a decade, left to be a full-time caregiver to her two children for just under two years. "I stayed very active in the bar. I kept my feet in things," Yonta says. She admits that her temporary leave was not a hindrance to re-entering the legal practice on her own terms, by starting her own law firm 20 months after leaving her assistant prosecutor position.

Beth A. Biedronski, a mergers & acquisitions attorney who left the law for three years to be home with her children, says that her time away from the law was a non-issue when she decided to rejoin the legal field. She had a solid record of experience closing deals prior to going to law school and had been with a prestigious D.C. law firm for eight years prior to her sabbatical. Biedronski reports that the three-year gap was not a hindrance in either her interview or her actual transition back to the law.

American Bar Association Past President Laurel Bellows left her successful Chicago law practice for one year to carry out her duties in the unpaid position of ABA president, before resuming her legal career in 2013.[2] She agrees that "[o]ne year is possible, longer risks loss of client relationships and rainmaking opportunities."

Put simply, if the time away is brief, it is unlikely to have a detrimental effect on your legal career. Nevertheless, there are ways to make the impact even more negligible.

## Make Friends with the Younger Kids on the Playground

iRelaunch's Carol Cohen points out that one of the most important things to do before and during a break from the law (or any career in fact) is to develop and maintain real, genuine relationships with the people who are/were junior to you when you leave/left.[3]

While you are on leave, these "junior" people will continue climbing the ladder, and may in fact be key to your reinstatement when you return. It is important to keep in touch with them during your break, keep them apprised of your accomplishments, and maintain a professional demeanor with them, with the goal that they continue to see you as a viable member of their professional team. By all means, brag about how refreshed you are by the break, but don't leave out information about the charity committees you are heading up or the *pro bono* case you took on this month. Over your every-so-often lunch meetings with the junior colleagues, ask for a report on a case they are handling, and mention a relevant update in the law based on a case reported in the professional journal to which you still subscribe.

## Keep Active in the Interim

Of course, to make these contacts with the once-junior lawyers meaningful, it will be important to make sure you head up a charity committee, take on a *pro bono* case, and subscribe to a few professional journals.

It does not have to be a charity committee. It can be any committee or organization, of course. But you have to head it up. Or co-head it. It would be best if the organization had a substantive financial or legal component to point to later. You also have to actively consider how your involvement in the organization could help further your career if and when you decide to relaunch down the road.

Carol Cohen notes how important it is that you "be very picky about what you take on." When choosing between a volunteer position with the local animal shelter or your children's school, it may be important to weigh the responsibilities, the budget at issue, the number of people you might be managing, and the tasks inherent in the position. In other words, you would serve your future professional goals well if you consider—*before* taking on a volunteer position—how that position can be articulated and presented in a job interview down the road.

Similarly, when subscribing to periodicals, consider titles other than *Men's Health* or *Vogue Magazine*. It goes without saying that "in addition to" is fine. But you should make sure to keep up your licenses, CLE requirements, and your subscription to the *Wall Street Journal*. And, by the way, the subscription will not be enough. You will have to force yourself to occasionally *read* the *Wall Street Journal*, and whatever it is you continue to subscribe to "in addition to" *Men's Health* or *Vogue Magazine*.

## The Rules Do Not Apply to You (For One Year at Least)

When I first planned my year-long sabbatical, I left on good terms, made sure there would be a job waiting for me at the end of the year, and spent exactly one year doing only what I wanted.

It was the year of "Me." I didn't return phone calls of people I didn't want to talk to and I didn't take on a single project that wasn't interesting to me. I took on many interesting projects, paying little attention to how little each one paid (if they paid at all). I paid even less attention to how each project would factor into my legal career down the road.

In many ways, it was the most productive year of my professional life.

So, I feel compelled to supplement that admittedly good advice—gleaned from the experts—that no matter how long you are taking off from the law, you should still dress up like a lawyer, have lunch with previously junior colleagues, and keep your legal skills fresh. You should still keep your mind's eye focused on the statistical possibility that you will at some time want to rejoin the legal field. But for Year One of any hiatus, you can exhale, because *none* of the rules apply to you.

Keep your license active. Take your required CLE courses.

Or don't.

Those are issues that are easy to fix after only one year. For year one, the world is your oyster.

There are rules and there are exceptions. And here's the thing. In discussing the general rules and lessons from experts in the fields of career counseling and legal recruiting herein, I have no intention of ignoring the exceptions. I embrace the exceptions.

I want *you* to be the exception to the rule.

I want *you* to take off as long as you need and resume your career—if you wish to—on your terms. Successfully. Measured by *your* terms of success.

So go ahead, take a year off. *A real year off.* Maybe more.

But just to be sure, it's a good idea while you're out to dip your toe back in the water occasionally.

## Keep Testing the Waters

After you transition from practicing, you should test the waters.

How? Simple. By scheduling pop quizzes for yourself.

Schedule regular lunches with people in the legal community: fellow lawyers, former mentors, and those junior colleagues who are steadily climbing past you on the seniority ladder while you continue on your sabbatical. Spend quality time with people you know will expect to talk about something other than the volunteer work, sports games, community, school events, and other issues that will most likely dominate the conversations you have with nonlawyers during your sabbatical.

Continue telling people at cocktail parties that you are a lawyer. Not that you *used* to be a lawyer. But that you *are* one. Still. Right now.

Let them know, subtly, that your caseload and client list total exactly zero, but do not dismiss the notion that you are indeed still a lawyer, and let them ask you the question *all* people love to ask lawyers: "Do you know a good lawyer who can help me/my brother/my Aunt Sue do X?"

It might not be you. This time. But you can refer them to a colleague who might be able to help, which will in turn keep you in the good graces of both your cocktail party companion *and* said lawyer, with whom you should immediately schedule lunch and talk *Wall Street Journal* or other professional-journal biz.

And maybe, just maybe, when you are ready to jump back into the legal waters, *you* will in fact be the "good lawyer" to whom you refer the next cocktail party or business lunch comrade.

## Notes

1. *Congress Avenue* Bridge, Bat Conservation International, http://www.batcon .org/index.php/our-work/regions/usa-canada/protect-mega-populations/cab-intro.

2. Laurel Bellows, Esq., Biography, American Bar Association, http://www .americanbar.org/groups/leadership/aba_officers/bellows.html.

3. Carol Cohen & Vivian Rabin, *Back on the Career Track: A Guide for Stay-at-Home-Moms Who Want to Return to Work* (Hachette Book Group USA, 2007), at 112.

## Chapter 3

# From Lawyer to Caregiver
## Making the Transition

*Do you miss being a lawyer?*
  *Yes, I do. I miss it. I really, really miss it.*
—Mother of four, who, at the time of interview, had been away from the
practice of law for about three years.

At first glance, it may seem counterintuitive to talk about a "transition" to caregiver status, when many lawyers juggle caregiving responsibilities alongside their active practices. Indeed, the decision to leave your paid position and become a full-time unpaid caregiver may not seem like a transition at all. To many, it may seem like a necessity.

There are certainly all types of caregivers, and lawyers (as do all professionals) often take leaves to care for sick family members or aging and/or ill parents. However, because such leaves are generally of the short-term "temporary" variety, I refer such transitioning attorneys to Chapter 2 (It's Only Temporary).

In this chapter, then, I'd like to address the type of transition to caregiver that more likely leads to a long-term, and sometimes even permanent, transition from the practice of law: the transition to stay-at-home parent. Although many lawyers who transition to full-time unpaid caregivers announce surprise that they made the decision, in fact statistics support the argument that their decision is neither novel nor aberrational.

According to some experts, including the late Suzanne Bianchi, a sociology professor at the University of California at Los Angeles and an expert in women's work and family choices, about one-third of married mothers leave the workforce to care for their children in any given year.[1] The Census Bureau counted 5.1 million stay-at-home moms in 2009, about 23 percent of all married mothers with children younger than 15 in their household.[2]

I found it interesting, after interviewing scores of transitioning attorneys over the years, that certain generalizations emerge. Here is one of them: Nearly every attorney who left the practice of law to be a full-time parent claimed to miss the law. This is in stark contradiction to the lawyers who transitioned to alternate legal careers or alternate careers altogether. The latter transitioning attorneys hardly ever said they missed law practice. In fact, in my experience, and as reported by *Life After Law* author Liz Brown, the latter transitioning attorneys generally claimed they wished they had done it much, much sooner.[3]

But not lawyers-turned-stay-at-home-parents. Mothers in particular. Whereas other transitioning attorneys rarely did, stay-at-home mothers admitted to missing the practice of law.

This assertion will be controversial, I have no doubt. Maybe because we do not want it to be true. I certainly did not want it to be true. I wanted to believe that those who had made the conscious, voluntary decision to leave the practice of law to become full-time caregivers would continue to embrace the decision without any longing and without any regrets.

But that does not seem necessarily to be the case.

This might be explained by two theories. The first holds that caregivers are "forced" out of the profession prematurely: That most of those attorneys who transition to full-time caregivers would have liked to find a way to reconcile their profession with their caregiver obligations. There are obvious flaws to this argument, of course. Certainly, there are examples of attorneys who want to juggle the practice of law with caregiving and who simply do so.

In *Back on the Career Track*, the co-authors and co-founders of iRelaunch, Carol Cohen and Vivien Rabin, detail the impressive career of attorney Ruth Reardon O'Brien (also known as the mother of comedian Conan O'Brien).[4]

O'Brien—who worked full-time while caring for six children—recalls that she managed by cutting out socializing outside of work hours and with carpools. "[My sense was] this is either going to be enormously successful or a huge failure."[5] She also relayed: "I used to come into the office a lot on Saturdays. But I'd always ask the kids who would want to come with me, and a couple of them always did. We'd bring a picnic lunch, and whoever came in got to have a conference room all to themselves where they would spread out all of their homework. The biggest draw was that each child who came got coins [for] the vending machines, which were a big deal back then. This worked for everyone."[6]

O'Brien's story is inspirational and certainly not isolated. The Mother Attorneys Mentoring Association of Seattle (MAMAS) is an organization founded in 2006 in an effort to empower attorney mothers and encourage them to succeed while celebrating their roles as attorneys and mothers. The group sponsors brown-bag lunches every month, featuring panel discussions addressing topics of particular interest to attorney mothers.[7]

The group, though originally founded in Seattle, now has sister organizations in seven cities/areas: Denver, Philadelphia, northern Virginia, Sacramento, Austin, Honolulu, and San Diego. Its celebration of mothers who have remained in the profession as lawyer moms is combined with the recognition that there are some who are contemplating alternatives:

> MAMAS aims to enhance the recognition of mother attorneys in the profession and community; promote the advancement of mother attorneys within the profession; facilitate the achievement of work-life balance; provide a forum for informing members and the legal profession about issues of particular concern to mother attorneys; facilitate the transition for attorney mothers who have taken time off and wish to re-enter the profession; support mother attorneys contemplating alternative work schedules or extended leaves of absence; and increase the interaction between mother attorneys of diverse backgrounds and practices.[8]

Putting aside for purposes of our present discussion the criticisms of law firm culture as conducive (or possibly not conducive) to work-life balance, the fact that there are indeed lawyer-parents who continue in the profession arguably belies the generalization that all attorneys who transition to full-time caregiving have no other choice. Indeed, anecdotally it appears that the attorneys who actually leave the practice of law to become full-time caregivers typically are the ones who were dissatisfied with the way they were practicing law in the first place. In a way, the caregiving responsibilities become if not the excuse, then certainly the *catalyst* for these attorneys to leave a profession that they were not enjoying.

In her book, *Opting In*, author/advocate Amy Richards proposes that women who leave their jobs to parent full-time are not leaving a wholly satisfying job. Rather, they are leaving one that did not in fact fulfill them.[9] Richards suggests that "[k]ids are a better excuse than admitting that your career ambitions changed, you are bored, you aren't as successful as you wanted to be, you want early retirement, you want to "take it easy," you are buying time before the next career move, or you don't really want to commute."[10]

Richards also argues that women who are *too* ambitious are more likely to leave. If you set out "to be Oprah by the time" you are 30, you might have no choice but to leave "rather than acknowledge failure in not being able to attain that level of success."[11]

Richards—of whom Gloria Steinem has said, "If her example and writing had been around earlier, even I might have had children"—also points out that women who have "more reasonable professional expectations at the outset . . . tend to find solutions that allow them to continue on professionally."[12]

In other words, it may well be that the lawyer moms who leave the practice of law are not the ones who are doing or achieving or completing what they want to be.

So why then do those lawyers miss it so much?

Well, consider a second theory: that caregiving is a much more demanding job than practicing law ever was. But that's not quite right either, as classifying caregiving as a "job" becomes a dangerous proposition for lawyers-turned-caregivers.

Certainly, it appears that lawyers-turned-caregivers miss the "idea" of what they left behind, a proposition that leads to one of the most difficult transitions of any we will explore herein.

And so, with this initial framework, we explore tips for transitioning to full-time unpaid caregiving. I note that the language in this section focuses on women/mothers because of the statistics and interview pool, with a recognition that men who leave the profession to become stay-at-home-dads may indeed face many, though not all, of the same issues.

1. Prepare to miss "it," but recognize the contradictions
2. Caregiving should not be your new "job"
3. Use the time
4. Cut costs—but not by firing the babysitter
5. Say yes more
6. Be good enough

## Prepare to Miss "It," but Recognize the Contradictions

While you may very well have left a job that was dissatisfying for many reasons, it is important to note that the catalysts prompting attorneys to leave to become full-time caregivers are more complicated than you think. Put simply, despite strides in the workplace, America is still a place where parenting and working are seen as mutually exclusive propositions.

Indeed, it is no secret that the United States lags far behind other industrialized nations in its protection of working families. Of 168 industrialized nations, the United States is one of only 5 without paid or subsidized maternity leave.[13] The passage of the Family and Medical Leave Act (FMLA) has been hailed as such a victory to American families, when in reality what American families need is not more unpaid leave, but rather protection of their jobs and *paid* leave. The bottom line is that there is strong support that American workplaces, including American law firms, are still places where parenthood—particularly motherhood—can be viewed as a liability to job performance.

Don't believe that's true?

Consider this: In nearly every state, it is still legal to ask a potential job candidate whether he or she is a single parent, and to exclude a candidate on that basis alone. This issue, nicknamed "maternal profiling," has garnered much attention in the press and notable journals, but little attention in the legislatures.

In the 1990s, Kiki Peppard became the poster child for the issue of maternal profiling, interviewed repeatedly by various national news outlets over the past two decades about her courageous and compelling story. A single mother trying to find work after her divorce, Peppard was repeatedly (and legally) turned down for administrative jobs after being asked (and answering honestly) that she was a single mother. After having to turn to welfare, Peppard finally obtained long-term employment years later—after the first interview where she was *not* asked about her personal family situation.

I interviewed Peppard in 2009 while on sabbatical from corporate law, and in 2010, I spent a significant period of time visiting legislators in her state—and my home state—of Pennsylvania in a vain attempt to recruit influential and motivated sponsors for legislation that had been drafted years earlier but had gone nowhere.

In 2010, I presented my research to the then-active Pennsylvania Commission for Women and told them about the then-pending stagnant bill HB 2245:

> I have been a corporate litigator for over 13 years, 10 of which have been spent at the most prestigious law firm in the country. I have negotiated multi-million dollar settlements, and tried my first case before I was 30. I have deposed and cross-examined fact and expert witnesses skillfully. Indeed, motions have been made, cases won, and settlements achieved on the bases of those depositions. I have argued numerous motions before federal and state judges (convincing judges to throw out jury verdicts, and convincing judges to throw out entire cases). I have successfully handled numerous special education cases, advocating on behalf of indigent clients who are trying to secure appropriate educational placement for their learning and/or behaviorally disabled children under federal and state laws. In fact, I was profiled for this work by the New York Lawyers for Public Interest in 2006. I have acted as special counsel for New York City and I have

taken depositions and helped develop trial strategy for cases brought against the City of New York.

Also, I have three children, ages 6, 4, and 2.

Why did I tell you that last piece of information?

Well, because I am not asking you to hire me. I wouldn't want you to know their ages, and I certainly wouldn't want you to know how many there are.

Because I've read the research. And I am well aware that motherhood—in this country, more than any other industrialized nation—is not viewed as a positive and certainly not as a qualification for the workforce.

The Commission's members were flabbergasted when I told them that parenthood was still a perfectly legal basis for discrimination in Pennsylvania and nearly all other state's job markets. We talked about the wage gap between men and women and about what we now know from many reputable sources to be true. The wage gap between men and women appears to be shrinking, narrowing.[14] Yet the wage gap between working mothers and the rest of the workplace population is not shrinking and is possibly growing.[15]

The startling truth is that women still make less than men in the workplace, and moms make *far* less.

Why is that? Well, there is research that sheds light on the cause of this problem, very specifically in the context of hiring and retention in the legal field. It demonstrates that mom lawyers are discriminated against and negatively stereotyped even before they begin working—even before they have a chance to work a single day. For example, in a study published in *Current Research in Social Psychology*, 135 lawyers looked at one of four résumés, in which each candidate had a similar background and education but one candidate was a mother, one a childless woman, one a dad, and one a childless man.[16] In the study, participants labeled on the questionnaire what specific criteria each candidate would have to meet to be hired. In other words, participants were asked what score/percentile ranking each applicant would need on a standardized ability test, what sorts of letters of reference, what type of LSAT score, and what percentage in his/her class each candidate would need to demonstrate in order to be hired as a first-year associate. Results suggested that mothers were negatively stereotyped and held to higher standards than childless women, and even fathers.[17]

When I was visiting legislators on numerous occasions to seek a vocal supporter for the stagnant House Bill 2245 (HB 2245), lawmakers were incredulous that such a gap existed in our discrimination laws. But they still failed to act. HB 2245 would have amended the Pennsylvania Human Relations Act (1955) to prohibit discrimination in employment based on marital or familial status, but such an amendment made many lawmakers that I talked to nervous about the "slippery slope." "You just don't touch the Pennsylvania Human Relations Act," I heard on more than one occasion. Of course, the executive director of the Pennsylvania Human Relations Commission had repeatedly confirmed the necessity of a bill banning maternal profiling because "there are employers within the Commonwealth who currently base their hiring, promotion, starting salaries, benefits offered and even termination decisions on whether an applicant is married, of child-bearing years or already has children."[18]

Some argue that no further legislation is necessary, as there are sex discrimination laws in place in every state—but of course these do not prohibit "maternal profiling." Consider: If an employer asks questions about marital and familial status of a woman, but not a man, and then refuses to hire the woman based on her marital or motherhood status, then discrimination *might* be proven under current laws. However, if an employer asks *both* men and women about their marital and familial status, and makes employment decisions based on that information, discrimination may not have occurred under the present law.

Note also that because there is no federal prohibition barring employment decisions from being based on marital or familial status, at least 63 other municipalities in 22 states have passed laws prohibiting discrimination based on marital or familial status. So it would seem that maternal profiling is indeed a very real issue in the workplace, including law firms. Coupled with the intense law firm culture, there is certainly an argument to be made that working parents—and lawyer moms in particular—would feel the effects of a bias that may very well act as a catalyst for leaving regardless of how they feel or enjoy the underlying job itself.

This is why it is important to recognize that transitioning from the law to become a full-time caregiver may very well bring with it a sense of longing and remorse for what could have been, had things only been different.

Which they were not.

The lawyer parents I spoke with talked about how they were unprepared to miss the law so much. Still, when probed, it generally appeared that what they missed was the *idea* of the career and not the career they had actually had.

Shannon Forchheimer, founder of the popular blog "But I Do Have a Law Degree," started out as your typical overachieving law school graduate. After graduating from the University of Pennsylvania Law School in 2005, where she served as a senior editor of the *Journal of Constitutional Law*, and interning for the Honorable Jerome B. Simandle of the United States District Court for the District of New Jersey, Forchheimer joined the New York City office of Skadden Arps as an associate in the litigation department, working on complex commercial litigations and government investigations involving RICO, federal securities laws, ERISA, and breach of contract. In 2007, Forchheimer relocated to Washington, D.C., and joined the government contracts department of Dickstein Shapiro.

In 2011, after the birth of her second son, Forchheimer left law firm life. In 2014, when I asked her "Do you miss any of it?" She answered easily: "Sure, I miss the camaraderie of having colleagues." "I miss the intellectual stimulation." "I miss going to work sometimes." And then Forchheimer made an admission: "I didn't quit for the kids . . . I quit for me. I quit because I wanted to be home."

In general, for most of the lawyers-turned-caregivers whom I interviewed, the inadequacies of the actual job and the desire to do something else ultimately combined with the issues of workplace bias and exhaustion to provide a catalyst for the decision to leave in these particular transitioning attorneys. Interestingly, the ability to resolve these feelings of remorse and regret seems directly proportional to how well and how much of the remaining steps outlined in this chapter each attorney employed into his or her own transition, including how in tune the attorney was with the inherent contradictions that arise from leaving.

Confidence struggles that arise when one is torn between responsibilities at the office and at home are replaced with new struggles, described almost universally by lawyers transitioning to full-time caregiving. I myself can vividly remember a moment from my first week of sabbatical in 2009, when I was doing the laundry on a Wednesday morning at 9:00 AM. A chore that I despise. A chore that I would rather outsource more than any others. Yet, as I was standing on the basement steps—laundry basket perched on my hip—I was suddenly filled with such happiness, I thought I would weep. I can remember the exhilaration like it was yesterday. I could do my family's laundry on a Wednesday morning at 9:00 AM without a competing legal brief deadline. Without worrying about what BlackBerry emails had stacked up in the time it had taken to catch the fabric softener cycle. I could fold the laundry carefully instead of rushing to catch a train. It was a symbolic moment.

It was also a moment that passed quickly.

Fast-forward six years, and I assure you that I have never again had any blissful moments of folding laundry at 9:00 AM on a Wednesday morning. Not one.

As Carol Cohen, co-founder of the consulting company iRelaunch, says, after voluntarily leaving her executive career to raise her children, she found herself wondering: "Why despite my education and experience, was I in the same place as women of a generation before me—the traditional volunteer/housewife."[19]

Cohen and I are not alone. In a 2013 *New York Times Magazine* article, Judith Warner, the *New York Times* best-selling author of *Perfect Madness*, noted a common finding among former professionals leaving for caregiving. It seemed that the formerly egalitarian roles of the household eroded as time went on; resentment was likely to occur not because of the caregiving responsibilities but because of the unequal delegation of responsibilities having to do with the household itself.[20]

"I had the sense of being in an unequal marriage," one of the interviewees told Warner. "I think he preferred the house to be 'kept' in a different kind of way than I was prepared to do it. If I had any angst about being an overeducated stay-at-home mom, it was not about raising the kids, but it was about sweeping."[21]

Indeed, when you spend some time reading the literature in this circle, it seems that no one is immune to the crisis of self that can occur with the transition to full-time caregiver. In the introduction to *The Price of Motherhood*, Pulitzer Prize nominee Ann Crittenden recounted: "A few years after I had resigned from the *New York Times* in order to have more time for my infant son, I ran into someone who asked 'Didn't you used to be Ann Crittenden?'"[22]

Put simply, the longing for an "ideal" career that never truly existed, the unequal delegation of the household responsibilities, and the angst over the attendant duties when all you have signed on for is "caregiver" are all common threads in the stories of transitioning attorneys who are now full-time caregivers, and often cause caregivers to report "missing" a job they left quite voluntarily, and with good reason.

It is helpful to keep all of this in perspective and to begin your transition to full-time caregiver with eyes wide open.

Will just the awareness of all of these struggles help?

Well, I remember one time swimming with my son in the Atlantic Ocean off the coast of South Carolina when he was suddenly stung by a jellyfish. It took me nearly a half hour to determine that the best course of treatment was a simple vinegar spray solution, something the mom-and-pop souvenir shop had on site. I went back and shared the solution with the lifeguard on duty, who protested that no one else had gotten stung by a jellyfish and that he didn't believe there were even jellyfish still in the nearby waters. "Humor me," I told him. "It's best to be prepared." He conceded my point with that line.

While neither I nor any of the transitioning attorneys I spoke with truly seemed to believe that the dissatisfaction (or at the very least, let's call it the feeling of the novelty of caregiving wearing off) could be avoided, as in all things, preparation seems critical to a successful transition. Prepare for the novelty to wear off, prepare for the dissatisfaction, and prepare for the exhaustion.

Don't believe any of those things will happen to *you*?

Humor me.

## Caregiving Should Not Be Your New "Job"

Beth A. Biedronski, attorney and mother of two, has an interesting (and relatable) story. After joining a start-up company after college, she was involved in more than 100 acquisitions, and decided to go to law school and ultimately do mergers and acquisitions work. After six years of practicing law with a top white-shoe law firm, including a couple of years when she had two small babies, Biedronski adjusted her schedule to one of part-time consulting work—and loved it. "I would have done that forever," she told me when we spoke in 2014. Unfortunately, after the economic crash of 2008, her firm could no longer keep up the part-time arrangement. Biedronski decided not to pursue full-time employment elsewhere, deciding instead to become a full-time caregiver to her two boys, then ages 2 and 4.

She was a full-time, at-home parent for three years before relaunching her career in 2011 with another law firm. Of her time away from the law, Biedronski says: "I think I was like many women who leave the law to stay at home. I poured every ounce of the previous energy I had devoted to my high-pressure, big law job to my new life. I was head of the pre-school PTA. If someone needed to drop off kids, they dropped them at my house. My house was immaculate, and my rugs constantly looked like they were brand new. If anyone needed anything, they came to me."

She also confessed, "It was exhausting."

Debra Vey Voda-Hamilton, founder of Hamilton Law & Mediation, agrees that transitioning attorneys—and particularly litigators—will have some difficulty keeping prior work habits from bleeding into the new life at home. Voda-Hamilton left the practice of law in 1996 and ultimately was away from the law for 13 years. During that time, she had leadership roles in various PTAs—but says she quickly learned that "we can't act as we did as litigators. You can't run roughshod over people like we did in litigation world, or they won't do anything, and then you'll be left to do things on your own."

Most, if not all, of the attorneys transitioning to full-time caregiving that I spoke to described a need to replace what they had left behind. Take Shannon Forchheimer, founder of the popular blog "But I Do Have a Law Degree," for example. After leaving her career, which included positions at New York's Skadden Arps and Washington, D.C.'s Dickstein Shapiro, Forchheimer left to take care of her two sons, and soon after started her blog, which has been voted one of the "Top 5 Lawyer Mom Blogs" by FindLaw's Legal Blog. After Forchheimer's blog was picked up by Above the Law, she began to be featured in numerous online publications, including *What's for Work?*, *The Washington Post*, *Montage Legal Group's blog*, and *Huffington Post Live*.

Forchheimer says she started the blog—which has been the stepping stone to many additional opportunities, including her most recent gig as lead Washington counsel for the successful freelance attorney group Montage Legal Group—as part of her post-transition struggle to address her changing identity. Although she is still not practicing full-time, she does take on freelance work with Montage Legal Group. "I wanted to have something interesting to talk about at cocktail parties." And not just any cocktail parties. Interestingly, her husband is a lawyer, and she attends firm functions with him. Forchheimer talks about how her husband's colleagues generally do not realize, until she tells them, that she is also a lawyer. (Forchheimer states unequivocally that she still considers herself to be an attorney and that she still identified herself as an attorney even before she took the freelance position with Montage Legal Group.)

Every year Forchheimer says she makes certain to put something new on her résumé, to avoid gaps and leave the door open for the potential of returning to full-time practice one day in the future. Forchheimer talks about her thoughtful plotting each year to ensure that her skills are sharp and her résumé is full. "Even though, to be honest, I don't know that I'll ever go back. The jury's still out."

Those "something new's" have included her blog and its resulting opportunities. Additionally, Forchheimer has courted the world of academia. Several years ago, she applied for a teaching position at George Washington University which did not pan out, but which did open the door to an online teaching position in the paralegal masters program. Also, since 2012 Forchheimer has been associated with the innovative company Montage Legal Group, which pairs highly credentialed lawyers with firms that need cost-effective project work.

Forchheimer respectfully disagrees with my opinion that caregiving should not be classified as a new "job" post-transition, and yet, despite our semantic disagreement, I cannot help but point to her successful transition from the practice of law to full-time caregiving as evidence that supports my opinion.

First of all, caregiving is *not* a job. A job has deadlines and some room for control and shaping. Parenthood, as you may already know, has none of that. And full-time parenthood? Even less. If you treat stay-at-home parenthood as a new job into which you need to pour all of your prior intensity, you will not be able to keep it up. And unlike your law career, which you really could leave when you burned out, parenthood is not a position you can leave due to burnout.

Plus, even though you see yourself as primary caregiver to the kids, you should not forget about throwing a little care the way of yourself. And your partner if you have one. In her best-selling book, *The Happiness Project*, lawyer-turned-author/happiness expert Gretchen Rubin points out that "Married people are so intertwined, so interdependent, that it's hard to maintain that sense of wonder and excitement."[23] She also notes the troubling fact that "studies show that married people actually treat each other with less civility than they show to other people."[24] Journalist Helen Kirwan Taylor once said: "In my view, making a child your career is a dangerous move because your marriage and sense of self can be sacrificed in the process."[25]

Second of all, caregiving probably *should not* be your job. I'm prepared to be criticized for this statement, but I stand by it. Hear me out.

Parenthood should be your vocation. You should take it seriously and you should love it and allow room to hate it sometimes too. But you should not make it your full-time "job." Leave room in your schedule for your other "jobs": volunteer work, part-time jobs, alternative jobs even. Though you may think in the beginning "I will never, ever, ever go back," statistics show that you should allow space for that decision to change over time, and you want to be thoughtful about your time off so that should you decide to relaunch later, it will be a less onerous process than it would be otherwise.

Indeed, statistics show that 93 percent of those who leave work to become full-time caregivers intend to return later to their careers.[26] While it is more likely to be the woman who leaves her career to parent, the average time that women take from their careers is only 2.2 years.[27]

It is important not to frame the relevant issues in terms of professional success or motherhood. Indeed, framing the relevant issue as one of choice between children and career can leave American parents, particularly moms, feeling marginalized. American lawyer moms? Even more so. And this all-too-common framing of the motherhood-versus-success "choice" for female lawyers in particular dismisses some amazing lawyer mom careers—not the least of whom is Justice Sandra Day O'Connor, of course.

Achieving the holy grail of a legal career, she was appointed as the first female Supreme Court Justice back in 1981. O'Connor's impressive résumé included positions in private practice, in the Arizona state senate, and on the state appeals court. She was also a mother of three. O'Connor did leave the law, albeit temporarily, for five years to raise her young children from 1960 to 1965. A choice? Sure. A choice between career and children? Not at all. O'Connor took a short hiatus from private practice after the birth of her second son and subsequently relaunched her legal career in 1965 by joining the Arizona Attorney General's office.[28]

O'Connor's story provides inspiration at every turn. Even though she graduated number three in the Stanford Law School class of 1952, she was deemed virtually unemployable and ended up starting her own general practice law office with a partner. In an interview with the *Back on the Career Track* authors, O'Connor joked that the type of walk-in client business she was handling at the time was "[n]ot exactly Supreme Court material."[29] When her second son was born in 1960, she left due to inadequate child care availability and stayed away from the profession for five years, until she joined the Arizona Attorney General's office in 1965. She tells the *Back on the Career Track* authors:

> With all the trouble I had had before, I was really worried that I would be unemployable, but I had to take care of those children. To keep my foot in the door, I realized I had to do something in the field even if it didn't pay. I wrote and graded bar exams for the state of Arizona, which kept me current in the law. I set up a lawyer referral plan for the local bar association, which was a good way to get acquainted with

other lawyers. I took a position on the county planning and zoning board and agreed to be a juvenile court referee. I also accepted some small bankruptcy appointments.[30]

O'Connor's description of a full plate of "work" while she was no longer "working" as a lawyer is not uncommon. In truth, the lines are blurred for attorneys who transition to caregiving in just the same way they are blurred for many parents in and out of the workforce. According to a *Washington Post* study cited by Amy Richards in *Opting In*, even women who identify themselves as "stay-at home" moms "are likely to have worked outside the home in the past year" and those who identify themselves as "working mothers" often work less than full-time.[31]

As Richards says: "I have witnessed this, too. There are non-working-outside-the-home women with full-time nannies who empathize with other full-time mothers as if they were one of them, yet also trump up something they are mildly working on, did work on, or plan to work on, all in order to blend in with mothers who work outside the home. Nothing could be clearer proof of our need for acceptance."[32]

Interestingly, in Salary.com's "Top 10 Reasons to Leave Your Job," parenting didn't even make the list.[33] Judith Warner's 2013 *New York Times Magazine* article cites a survey by Sylvia Ann Hewlett (economist and founding president of the Center for Talent Innovation in New York) polling thousands of women in 2004 and after the financial crisis in 2009. Hewlett's survey found that about 33 percent of "highly qualified women" leave their jobs to spend extended time at home, and about 73 percent of those return to work.[34]

To sum it up simply, keep in mind during your hiatus as full-time caregiver that you may indeed want your old "job" back some day. Parent your children with the same earnestness you have from Day One, but don't make parenting your new "job." As Richards points out in *Opting In*, "It doesn't have to be an either/or, but rather 'one and then the other.'"[35]

## Use the Time

Erin Giglia is co-founder of Montage Legal Group, a nationwide network of experienced, highly credentialed freelance attorneys, and works with hundreds of women who have transitioned from the practice of law to focus on caregiving. Giglia says that she advises women leaving the law to make no big decisions for about six months. She says that she often tells potential candidates for the Montage Legal Group to give themselves the time to "re-connect" with their family and friends and, most importantly, to "re-connect with their lives."

She says that when she consults with an attorney who is thinking about transitioning from the full-time practice of law, she makes certain universal recommendations. "First, you have no idea how you are going to feel until you leave. Don't assume you know what you will be able to take on, and what you will be able to say no to."

Her advice is to take about six months—what she calls a "real break"—to do the work that needs to get done. "You need to get over this weird kind of PTSD you will have. You need to give up bad habits, like eating lunch at your desk."

This is great advice. As I have mentioned, my first year off was my own version of a "happiness project" (and this was even before I read Gretchen Rubin's meme).

In her sequel to *New York Times* best-seller *The Happiness Project*, Gretchen Rubin notes that "[a] guiding principle for all who undertake a happiness project is 'first, do no harm.'"[36] She also notes the fundamental paradox of life: "The days are long, but the years are short."[37] Many attorneys transitioning to caregiving find that this principle applies to their new life at home just as much as it did to the life at the office that they are leaving behind. Another way of looking at this theory is: "Our lives live in the naïve notion that later there will be more room than in the entire past."[38]

Amy Gewirtz, director of the New Directions for Attorneys program at Pace Law School for relaunching attorneys, agrees, and cautions against losing sight of the need for constant self-evaluation. She notes that leaving the law is a very emotional time, and it is important to clear your head—but it is also important to continually do self-assessment.

Because the identity issues inherent in any transition from the practice of law seem magnified when transitioning to full-time caregiving, the advice from experts to self-reflect, to remember self-care, and to use the time seems particularly poignant here.

## Cut Costs—but Not by Firing the Babysitter

Financial considerations become obvious stressors for many lawyers transitioning to caregiving. Losing an entire salary is rarely an insignificant event for a family.

As Liz Brown, author of *Life After Law*, told me, it would be nice advice to tell transitioning attorneys to "try it out" first. Try living on less money for a significant period of time, such as six months or a year—but that, of course is generally not practical or possible."

The good news is that the very reason it is not practical or possible is that you necessarily spend money while you are immersed in firm life that you simply will not need to spend later on. Conveniences like take-out food and dry cleaning will fall away dramatically when and if you transition from the practice. Transportation and commuting costs may be greatly diminished as well. Perhaps the most dramatic category of expense that will disappear if you leave firm life—particularly big firm life—is the category I call "self-soothing." These are the expenses that nearly every attorney admits to incurring while practicing law: Expensive meals, clothes, vacations, and *things* that are often unnecessary (and indeed often go unappreciated) but are accumulated in an attempt to comfort dissatisfied lawyers who feel entitled to spend the money they are working such long hours to earn.

Not all of the expenses will simply disappear, of course. You will need to be proactive about cutting many expenses. You may have to downsize your home, your car, and/or your children's extracurricular expenses. On the one-year anniversary of the start of my sabbatical from Skadden Arps, my husband and I closed on a home in a Pennsylvania town that we deliberately chose for its quality-of-life aspects, including a lower cost of living than our previous town in Long Island, New York.

Not everyone can move, obviously, but as Shannon Forchheimer, founder of the award-winning "But I Do Have a Law Degree" blog, says, she regrets not considering the possibility of transitioning to caregiving when purchasing her home. She would have considered "less" home for "less" money. In fact, she says, "I definitely could have used more childcare help . . . but felt the expense was too big when I first left my job."

Indeed, the tension between the need for more child care and the need to cut costs is a commonly reported one. Hollee Temple, co-author of *Good Enough Is the New Perfect* (Harlequin 2011), says that when she left the practice of law, she gave up too much child care. She hired students and gave up her full-time babysitter, but she lacked consistency and in hindsight says it really was not enough.

While it may be a necessity to cut back on third-party child care, it is an important issue to reconsider at the beginning of the transition. Not whether to have any child care, but how to obtain it. Before giving up your full-time or part-time babysitter, consider, as some of the lawyer moms I talked to did, whether your babysitter can continue in a family-share arrangement. If you have a cleaning service *and* a babysitter, consider whether one person can take over both tasks for a lower weekly/monthly household expense. Alternatively, decide whether your high-priced nanny might be replaced by a lower-charging college student who is available consistently for a few hours each week. How about a babysitting co-op with your neighbors or friends, where each mom takes a turn watching a few children at her home weekly, while the other moms have an opportunity to run child-free errands or pursue other activities? Are there any family members who can provide some cheap and regular babysitting?

Casey Berman, former practicing attorney and founder of the "Leave Law Behind" blog, has some practical tips for focusing on and heading off financial concerns at the outset of a transition.[39] As Casey points out: "[O]ne of the main obstacles lawyers face in leaving law behind is a fear around money: A fear of the unknown, a fear of a lack of financial literacy, a fear of facing their bad spending habits, a fear of having the 'money talk' with their spouse, a fear that they can't make money in any way other than being an attorney, a fear that if they leave their job as an attorney they'll soon be financially ruined."[40]

Berman suggests that would-be transitioning attorneys attempt to clearly define their monthly "cash burn rate" by looking at month-to-month spending over the past two years. Berman suggests a conservative approach: "Take the average expenses of the four highest months (over this two-year period) and multiply this average by one to two years. This is the baseline expense number for you to work with moving forward."[41]

Once the monthly burn rate is established, Berman suggests lining up some part-time work or paid sabbatical time, even before leaving—a safety net of sorts. In addition, accurately determine assets, cash, savings, any lines of credit, and any other readily available sources of cash. Remember that freelance attorney work can be a highly lucrative (though erratic and therefore potentially unreliable) source of income.[42] Berman also pragmatically suggests that "if you come to the conclusion that you have little or no safety net, then it may prove beneficial to stay at your job for another year or two and sock away money (all the while developing the rest of your blueprint to leave the law behind)."[43]

The point is, if there are other areas to cut, don't make babysitting the first one, and especially do not do this because you have resolved that babysitting is to be your new job. (Unless you are actually charging for babysitting through co-op shares or other currency, in which case then babysitting *is actually* your new job. In no other instances should it be.)

Are you wondering why you would need a babysitter or any third party to help with caregiving—the very task you are leaving the practice of law to do? Easy.

Although caregiving is going to continue to be the vocation it always was—you may very well consider adding dimensions to your life.

What things?

All the things you are going to say "Yes" to.

Which sounds dangerous—and it can be—so follow along.

## Say Yes More

After about a year away from the practice of law, a year of saying "yes" to so many things I had never been able to say yes to previously—mid-morning coffee meetings, volunteering, multiple board positions, freelance work, body combat class on a Wednesday morning, teaching art history to elementary students—I began to wonder if perhaps I should start saying no more. Certainly, that becomes a popular response after being home for a year or two:

"Just say no to more things."

"I really need to start saying no."

What I have learned from transitioning from the practice of law and interviewing dozens of transitioning-to-caregiving attorneys about all the things they say yes and no to is that our problem is *not* that we say yes too much, but rather too little.

About two years into my transition from the practice of law, I found myself chairing a fundraising committee. I had been asked. I said yes. It seemed like a logical cause and effect. But I was new in town, and asked a woman who seemed much more connected than I if she would be interested in helping me out. Make phone calls. Make connections for me.

She said, "You know, I'm working on saying no more. I'm going to start now."

I wasn't offended. I had said yes to quite a few things since my sabbatical commenced. I started to question whether I said yes too much—for no other reason than I began hearing people say they "should" say no more.

"No" became the new black.

I almost started to believe it myself.

That is, until the day I accidentally joined a vegan cooking club, even though I am not vegan, and soon thereafter developed my theory that what transitioning attorneys really need is to say yes more.

*Accidentally? But how—?*

Actually, it was easier than you might think. A few years into my sabbatical from the practice of law and new in town—read: lonely—I gratefully accepted an invitation from a local philanthropic group for coffee and a speaker. At some point over coffee, after I mentioned that we had moved from New York, my hostess pulled me aside.

"I moved from New York a few years ago too—you'll find new places to shop, don't worry," she teased warmly. Then: "Hey, I've just started a new cooking club—you should—"

"Absolutely. Yes. Sign me up."

Obviously amused by my quick response, my hostess winked and smiled, leaning in to whisper: "I should tell you . . . we cook vegan . . . and no sugar."

I stepped back quickly, afraid she'd smell the cream-filled donut I had for breakfast still on my breath. "That's great!" I replied ridiculously, searching my brain, trying to remember what *vegan* actually meant. No meat, obviously, but what else would we *not* be cooking?

Over the next few months, I discovered very quickly what we *would* be cooking: marinaded tofu, creamy soups made with a millet base instead of dairy, chocolate mousse created from avocados. (Yes, avocados.) Eventually, we stopped calling it a "Vegan Club," and started calling it "Healthy Cooking Club" instead. (As my vegan-club-founding friend still laments monthly: "I hate the V word. Why do we have to qualify everything we make with that word? Why can't it just be chocolate? Or soup? Or mousse? Or lasagna?")

Why indeed?

Sure, the whole experience changed the way I look at food. Before I accidentally joined the cooking club, I knew generally that cupcakes belonged on the "not healthy" side of the nutrition equation and that carrot sticks belonged on the "healthy" side. But I had no idea how to pronounce *quinoa* and had never voluntarily eaten kale. I'm still not vegan. I'm more like a vegan-who-eats-meat-and-dairy. (Why do we have to qualify everything with the V word anyway?)

Mostly, what accidentally joining the vegan cooking club really taught me was how to connect with people again. People who are seemingly not like me, who then show me every month how much we share, and how much we can learn from each other. Like the freezing point of coconut oil (76 degrees Fahrenheit, of course). What bad habits we all can un-learn together. (Sugar. Processed everything.) And the best places in town to find last-minute gifts for a 10-year-old's birthday party.

*Connection.*

As Montage Legal Group co-founder Erin Giglia rightfully pointed out, lawyers are notoriously unconnected from other people—and from their own lives. Sure, it may seem like a stereotype, but it is also a fact. Or so I've found. Giglia says: "You are going to have to take some time. It's like having a baby. Even though you think you know what it will be like. You don't. You don't know until you actually do it. And the same is true with transitioning from the practice of law."

You'll need, in short, to learn how to reconnect with your life.

In fact, every "yes" gives you the opportunity to decide for yourself what the next path should be. It helps you weed out the things you don't want to do, and opens up opportunities to do things you might indeed want to do long term. As Giglia says—contrary to what some will tell you—"luck" *does* have a part in success: You never really know who you are talking to and what opportunities will present themselves after a conversation. Likewise, you never really know whether what you are saying yes to will lead to a dream come true down the road.

Think you don't—or won't—have time?

Well, I'll tell you. I'm asked all the time how I fit so much into my day. As I edited this chapter, I was literally sitting in the car in a restaurant parking lot after finishing a valuable telephone interview from 12:15 to 12:45 with a transitioning attorney for this very book. I had a lunch meeting in the restaurant for a volunteer committee that I headed up at the time, and I left that meeting to conduct a 2:00 PM conference call in my car for ShopFunder, the start-up company of which I was vice president at the time.

Crazy? Maybe.

But how different is this from the billable-hours model we operated under for so long, where every hour was efficiently accounted for? Where different matters tugged at us during the day, calling for us to change hats depending upon the hour, depending upon the client? It is my experience that if you use your billable-hour training for good, you will find that you can pack a lot more into your day. Of course, as Claire Cook says in her best-selling book, *Never Too Late: Your Roadmap to Reinvention*, there is a fine line between saying yes to many valuable endeavors, and a "bad case of shiny object syndrome."[44]

How do you decide what things to say yes to? For starters, it should be the things that move and compel *you*. Not the things you *think* you should say yes to.

I remember when I first took a sabbatical from the law, my oldest had just started kindergarten and my middle child had started preschool. I had never had any time to linger at the school after dropoff, and I found myself doing just that: "lingering." Meeting the staff, looking at artwork hanging on the wall, spending a little extra time at the door to say goodbye to my son as he left, time that had suddenly become important to *me*, and not to my kids at all.

One day the preschool teacher pulled me aside and said, "I have a question for you. Would you be interested in being our class mom this year? I think you'd be great."

You could have knocked me over with a feather.

I was elated. Truthfully, I'm not even sure I knew what a "class mom" was. And I certainly didn't know that I'd be "great" at it, but the fact that someone else thought there was something in my new role that I might actually be great at was enough of a confidence boost for me. I eagerly signed on and organized teacher gifts, wrangled classroom volunteers, and drafted communication to the other classroom parents all year long.

The next year, in a new school, I volunteered myself to be class mom for multiple classrooms. And team mom for the kids' tee ball team, and—oh, about 10 other volunteer positions. Until one night, while I was watching my son's hamster's overblown cheeks, puffed with food, while I cleaned out his cage, I actually started talking to him out loud.

"I too may have bitten off more than I can chew, Nibbles."

Although I said this, I wasn't thinking about the fact that my son was getting old enough to clean out his own hamster's excrement or that I was wasting my time talking to a small rodent. I was looking at Nibbles' enlarged pouches full of the food he had stored away earnestly and empathizing. "Smaller bites would be better, Nibbles."

I had taken on a host of volunteer duties, including hamster cages, that were not necessarily important to *me*. And therein lay my mistake. The next year, I successfully pared down to the positions that *were* most important to *me*. The board positions where I felt I could make the biggest impact, class mom for the child who needed me in the classroom the most each year, and fundraising for local groups that moved me personally. Employing the "these are my new billable hours" mentality, I was able to fit quite a bit of volunteering in, alongside a full-time position as VP of a newly rebranded start-up company, even when some asked "Shouldn't you just start saying no more often?" The wonderful by-product of saying yes to more quality projects is that it will be unnecessary to say no to the rest. Your time will fill itself up.

Still think you don't have time, even though you used to work under the stringent billable-hours regime? Try putting yourself on a small but consistent deadline for a project and see how much you can get done. Claire Cook, who also wrote the best-selling *Must Love Dogs*, tells how she writes two pages per day every day.[45]

> When I'm writing a novel, I write two pages (Times New Roman, 12 point, double-spaced, single sided) a day, seven days a week. . . . No matter what is or isn't happening in my life, I can write two pages a day. Consistently. Day in and day out. And at the end of five or six months, even factoring in a few inevitable *I just can't do it any more* meltdowns, I have the first draft of a book.[46]
>
> So figure out your own version of my two pages a day.[47]

More importantly, figure out the thing you want to spend two pages per day on. That thing that pulls at you day and night. That thing that you find yourself thinking about, maybe even trying out in conversation with your best friends. That thing that finishes your "I would have loved to do _____" sentence. If you haven't found "it" yet, use your time to do so.

In the end, my argument for saying yes more is supported by some of my own favorite things to dedicate two pages per day to: writing, my vegan cooking club, and my volunteer involvement with a group called "Art Goes to School," as well as an unlikely lesson from my kids.

Art Goes to School is a volunteer effort to bring reproductions of famous artwork into our children's elementary schools and teach them about the history and importance of art in our world. When I first began volunteering for the program, I wondered just how I would tackle that job with my children's kindergarten and second-grade classrooms. How to convince 5- to 8-year-olds of the importance of Delacroix and Eakins? Artists who were not even really understood in their own lifetimes?

I stumbled upon the answer one night.

After I kissed the kids and tucked them into bed, I heard the boys reading out loud in their respective bedrooms to their hamsters. One had gotten the idea and the other followed. When I checked on them, my 7-year-old exclaimed, "Nibbles is nocturnal, Mom, so he loves when I read to him at night." His smile and pride were infectious.

I couldn't help but be happy that he was reading aloud to a rodent. Because if I know anything from my transition from the law, it's that sometimes it's important to do things that are beautiful and meaningful—even if they are only beautiful and meaningful to you.

Like art.

Like reading bedtime stories to a hamster.

The secret to successful "Yes"-ing is to figure out what are your bedtime stories for hamsters and what are your "bright shiny objects"—and then say yes to the former.

## Be Good Enough

From my own experience, and from interviewing transitioning attorneys, I have learned how tempting it is to believe that—when you transition to full-time caregiver and you can pour all of your energy into the task—you will be very close to perfect.

Hollee Schwartz Temple and Becky Beaupre Gillespie, co-authors of *Good Enough Is the New Perfect,* describe the phenomenon of moms, including lawyer moms, who have "professionalized motherhood . . . filling their planners with swimming/music/dance lessons and playgroups where the hostess mothers routinely decorated cupcakes (peanut-free, of course) with each child's first initial."[48] "Yes, it's sometimes an exhausting dance . . . . But it can also be a thrilling one, especially when we feel satisfied and successful and in control."[49]

Temple and Gillespie state that "[t]o fully understand the New Perfect, we need to understand more about who we are, where we came from and how the progress we inherited as modern women has given us both our greatest gifts and our most intractable challenges."[50] Taking a hard look at the so-called "Opt-Out Revolution," Temple and Gillespie say that "[s]omewhere in the middle of the chaos and crisis, something new began to emerge. The Baby Boomers' daughters began piecing together three generations' worth of dreams. We examined what we wanted and mapped out how to get it. We rethought what it meant to Have It All, and we abandoned the stuff that didn't work."[51] Herein began to be room for the "Good Enoughs"—those who recognize what, according to Temple and Gillespie, "we all should have known all along: We would never really Have It All. Not in the traditional sense anyway."[52]

In 2013, Temple started the Beauty Bar, a natural extension of her "Good Enough" brand, which preaches that caregivers are valuable and need to make time for themselves. The Beauty Bar is a full-service salon and day spa that offers complimentary child care to mothers taking advantage of salon services every Monday morning. In fact, Temple says, many of her clients are lawyer moms, and she likens her business to a "ministry"; she encourages her staff to see it that way as well. And indeed, Temple's determination to build up the Beauty Bar—"It seems I'm trying to achieve the opposite of work-life balance, right?" Temple joked when we spoke in the summer of 2014—is based on her own hard-fought battle against insecurities with her mothering both while still working and after leaving her law career. "Because no matter how confident we are in our choices, deep down, we all want to be perfect mothers."[53]

And yet, as Temple and Gillespie reveal—and of course as we knew all along—just as we knew we couldn't really have it all, the myth of perfect motherhood is just that: *a myth.*

Better to be real than a myth.

Better to be good enough.

## Notes

1. Katherine Reynolds Lewis, *The Return: A Stay-at-Home Mom Attempts to Go Back to Work after Nearly Two Decades. Can She Revive Her Career?*, Wash. Post (April 4, 2010).

2. *Id.*

3. Liz Brown, J.D., *Life After Law* (Massachusetts: Bibliomotion, 2013), at xiii.

4. Carol Cohen & Vivian Rabin, *Back on the Career Track: A Guide for Stay-at-Home-Moms Who Want to Return to Work* (Hachette Book Group USA, 2007).

5. *Id.* at 186.

6. *Id.* at 187.

7. http://www.mamaseattle.org.

8. *Id.*

9. Amy Richards, *Opting In: Having a Child Without Losing Yourself* (Farrar, Straus & Giroux, 2008), at 20.

10. *Id.* at 20–21.

11. *Id.* at 22.

12. *Id.*

13. *Id.* at 35 (citing Jody Heymann, Alison Earler, Stephanie Simmons, Stephanie M. Breslow, & April Kuehnhoff, *The Work, Family, and Equity Index: Where Does the United States Stand Globally* [The Project on Global Working Families, June 16, 2004]).

14. *Id.* at 39-40.

15. *Id.*

16. Fuegen et al., *Evidence of Shifting Standards in Judgments of Male and Female Parents' Job-Related Ability*, 15 Current Res. in Soc. Psych., no. 5 (May 22, 2010).

17. *Id.*

18. *See, e.g.*, Pennsylvania Human Relations Commission, *Annual Reports* (2003-2004, 2002-2003, 2001-2002).

19. Carol Cohen & Vivian Rabin, *Back on the Career Track: A Guide for Stay-at-Home-Moms Who Want to Return to Work* (Hachette Book Group USA, 2007), at 4.

20. Judith Warner, *The Opt-Out Generation Wants Back In*, N.Y. Times Magazine (August 7, 2013), http://www.nytimes.com/2013/08/11/magazine/the-opt-out-generation-wants-back-in.html?pagewanted=all&_r=0.

21. *Id.*

22. Ann Crittenden, *The Price of Motherhood* (Picador, 2010).

23. Gretchen Rubin, *The Happiness Project* (Harper Paperbacks, 2011), at 63.

24. *Id.* at 67.

25. Amy Richards, *Opting In: Having a Child Without Losing Yourself* (Farrar, Straus & Giroux, 2008), at 22.

26. *Id.* at 16.

27. *Id.*

28. Carol Cohen & Vivian Rabin, *Back on the Career Track: A Guide for Stay-at-Home-Moms Who Want to Return to Work* (Hachette Book Group USA, 2007), at 177-79.

29. *Id.* at 179.

30. *Id.*

31. Amy Richards, *Opting In: Having a Child Without Losing Yourself* (Farrar, Straus & Giroux, 2008), at 18-19.

32. *Id.* at 19.

33. *Id.* at 20.

34. Judith Warner, *The Opt-Out Generation Wants Back In*, N.Y. Times Magazine (August 7, 2013), http://www.nytimes.com/2013/08/11/magazine/the-opt-out-generation-wants-back-in.html?pagewanted=all&_r=0.

35. Amy Richards, *Opting In: Having a Child Without Losing Yourself* (Farrar, Straus & Giroux, 2008), at 16.

36. Gretchen Rubin, *Happier at Home: Kiss More, Jump More, Abandon Self-Control, and My Other Experiments in Everyday Life* (Three Rivers Press, 2012), at 6.

37. *Id.* at 13.

38. *Id.* at 129-30.

39. Casey Berman, *From the Career Files: The First Step in Leaving Law Behind—It's the Money, Stupid*, Above the Law (January 14, 2013), http://abovethelaw.com/career-files/the-first-step-in-leaving-law-behind-its-the-money-stupid.

40. *Id.*

41. *Id.*

42. *Id.*

43. *Id.*

44. Claire Cook, *Never Too Late: Your Roadmap to Reinvention* (Marshbury Beach Books, 2014), at 26.

45. *Id.* at 37.

46. *Id.*

47. *Id.* at 39.

48. Becky Beaupre Gillespie & Hollee Schwartz Temple, *Good Enough Is the New Perfect: Finding Happiness and Success in Modern Motherhood* (Harlequin, 2011), at 16.

49. *Id.* at 21.

50. *Id.*

51. *Id.* at 28.

52. *Id.*

53. *Id.* at 57.

# Chapter 4

# Discipline, Disbarment, and Other Involuntary Exits from the Practice of Law

*You have to be able to articulate in 20 words or less what you have done wrong. And then you have to be able to articulate in 20 words or less what you have done to make it right. You must have integrity . . . and humility. Because once you have made peace with your past, everyone else can also.*

—Samuel Bellicini, reinstated to the practice of law in 2008, after a 1994 resignation with charges pending.

In 1997, I was assigned to a case in which two men were injured while cleaning paintbrushes with gasoline next to a hot water heater with an open flame. The men were lucky to be alive, and lucky to have all their limbs functioning and intact. But they had suffered—and healed from—some very serious burns, which formed the basis of their damages lawsuit against many parties, including the landlord and the company that maintained the hot water heater.

While it was arguable that no warnings should have been needed against the potential for injury while washing paintbrushes with gasoline, let alone near an open flame, there were indeed warnings—plenty of them. They were printed in various shapes and sizes and affixed all over the hot water heater. But the adequacy of the warnings were an issue in the case, complicated by the fact that the men claimed to speak no English, and the written warnings were printed in English.

I was scheduled to take one of the men's depositions one afternoon in opposing counsel's office. I arrived on time, but opposing counsel had over-scheduled his afternoon and left me in his office waiting room for what seemed a very long time. He also left his client sitting in the same waiting room, as well as the interpreter hired for the deposition. I worked on my deposition outline while I waited. The interpreter sat quietly, and the plaintiff leafed through an issue of *Time* Magazine.

When we were all finally called into the deposition room, I asked my first question, looking directly at the plaintiff while the interpreter interpreted.

"Mr. P, do you read any English?"

He waited for the interpretation, answered in his native language, and then the English response came back via the interpreter.

"No."

"Mr. P, why then were you reading *Time* Magazine in the waiting room of your attorney's office for the last half hour?"

I thought I saw a flicker of recognition in the plaintiff's eye. It was brief, though, as the response finally came back via the interpreter.

"I understand no English at all. I was merely looking at the pictures."

"You can understand pictures, then, right, Mr. P?"

"Of course."

"Well, can you tell me what this picture means, Mr. P?"

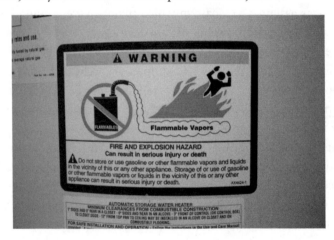

This time, Mr. P didn't wait for the interpretation to look crestfallen. I looked over at the attorney, who nodded a little concession to me.

We finished the deposition quickly. The case ended favorably for my client shortly thereafter.

The bottom line was that Mr. P clearly had been hurt. But he also had made a mistake. And the truth in law and life is that you don't always get to blame someone else for your mistakes.

Sometimes, you have to move on. Sometimes the past really does have to stay right there—in the past.

In the summer of 2014, I spoke with Samuel Bellicini about his journey to reinstatement to the practice of law. He started our conversation bluntly, asking, "Do you want to hear about the years before I was disbarred?"

"But you weren't disbarred, right? Didn't you resign?" I asked him.

"I resigned with charges pending. It's the same thing. It's the exact. Same. Thing." In a decision during Bellicini's reinstatement proceeding, the Review Department confirmed this to be true: "Although petitioner resigned with disciplinary charges pending, he must meet the same requirements for readmission as if he were disbarred." *In re Bellicini* (citing *In re Rudman* (Review Dept. 1993), 2 Cal. State Bar Ct. Rptr. 546, 552).

Bellicini is above all honest and repentant. He is not soft or a pushover. He makes no excuses, and does not embellish the facts. He demands the same from others.

When I introduced myself and explained that I had been a litigator for 13 years "in Manhattan," with added emphasis on the last 4 syllables, he interrupted to point out: "You know, Amy, it doesn't make your 13 years of practice more impressive because you were *in Manhattan*." He stressed the same four syllables and I realized for the first time how silly I sounded.

We laughed together and he shared a lot more wisdom with me. The kind of wisdom that you would expect from a man whose reinstatement to the practice of law 15 years after his "disbarment" was the result of a hard-fought battle to regain sobriety and integrity. I try out his wisdom when I speak with other attorneys who have left the practice of law involuntarily, and they agree that his words ring true. Three core principles keep rising to the top, and those are the ones Bellicini agrees should make the cut here.

1. Accept that you cannot change the past
2. Articulate in 20 words or fewer what you have done to make "it" right
3. Stage your comeback

## Accept That You Cannot Change the Past

When he was deposed in connection with his first reinstatement trial in 2005, Bellicini recalls that the deposing attorney asked him a series of difficult questions. "Mr. Bellicini, are you an alcoholic?" "Mr. Bellicini, did you steal money from Client A?" Each time, Bellicini explains that he answered simply, "Yes."

"And each time I answered honestly, she [the deposing attorney] would look down and cross out an entire page of subsequent questions."

"You can't change the past," Bellicini states prophetically. More than that, he points out, when you stop trying to change the past—when you stop trying to make excuses for the past—you get unstuck from it.

You can move forward, and people will cross out entire pages of subsequent questions.

George (name changed at the request of the interviewee) agrees with this way of thinking. George—a government-employed attorney who was forced into retirement early—admits that in the beginning, he really struggled. "I think I was mostly embarrassed," he says. But then a former colleague gave him some wonderful advice that he says has made all the difference: "He said 'Let it go.' And I'm really working on that."

## Articulate in 20 Words or Fewer What You Have Done to Make "It" Right

Bellicini's dreams of being a trial attorney started in his teen years. After being held up—not once, but twice—as a Taco Bell assistant manager at

16 ("I was literally begging for my life"), Bellicini got a job as a file clerk for an attorney/mentor, who took Bellicini under his wing. The mentor taught Bellicini how to shepardize cases, update the looseleaf Matthew Bender binders, and even allowed Bellicini to sit alongside him at counsel table during trials.

Bellicini says that from that time on, he wanted to do nothing else but practice law. In fact, he was admitted to practice in 1991, but by then he had a serious problem with alcohol. After a series of positions, including running his own general practice firm, he tendered his resignation from the practice of law to a state bar representative in 1993, with charges pending.[1]

"I responded to the state bar inquiry because I had no job and nothing else to do at the time. The investigator told me he would not let me out of his office until I resigned . . . . He actually did me a favor. A big favor."

The resignation was not exactly rock bottom for Bellicini. In fact, he did not get sober until 2001—more than six years after his resignation—but in the meantime, Bellicini sought out temporary jobs through a reputable temp agency, focusing on law-related jobs (including calendar clerk and file clerk positions for various firms). On May 15, 2001, after his wife made what he calls "a credible threat" to leave with their son, Bellicini got sober, and began seeking intensive counseling and support to ensure that sobriety stuck.

In 2003, he took a temp job as a secretary in the legal department of the Post Office, and eventually became a paralegal there, working on summary judgment motions, and carving out a niche for himself. After about three years of being sober, Bellicini says he began to think seriously about reinstatement. He began making amends and restitution, and most importantly, sought outside help to stay sober—through counseling, groups, and the Other Bar (http://www.otherbar.org/), an organization of recovering lawyers and judges that provides support to members of the legal profession with substance abuse problems. Bellicini credits the Other Bar as being instrumental not only in his reinstatement to law, but also to his continued sobriety as well.[2]

Bellicini's own "20 words" include ones such as "commitment to sobriety," "restitution," and "amends." In an Order dated 2006, the court noted that "Petitioner accepted full responsibility for the ethical misconduct he committed prior to his resignation and expressed remorse for the harm he caused his former clients as a result of his inability to represent them properly."[3] The court also detailed Bellicini's road to recovery beginning with his first day of sobriety in 2001, his enrollment in a two-year chemical dependency recovery program (CDRP) offered through Kaiser Permanente, almost daily group therapy sessions, and weekly individual visits with a psychologist, which he later supplemented with regular recovery group meetings and weekly meetings of the Other Bar.[4]

In 2008, after two trials and a lengthy battle for reinstatement that has become precedent for matters Bellicini himself now argues in his practice before the California State Bar Court, Bellicini was reinstated to the practice of law. He had indeed successfully articulated just how he had "made it right."[5]

## Stage Your Comeback

If Bellicini's story is an example, the road to comeback is neither easy nor fast, and may require more than a little humility along the way.

Despite Bellicini's initiation of proceedings in 2003, he was not reinstated until 2008. In fact, his first trial did not result in reinstatement despite overwhelming evidence *in favor of* the case for reinstatement. The court at that time noted the testimony of a key witness for Bellicini, Dr. Kate Riley, a clinical psychologist and petitioner's treating medical professional:

> [P]etitioner is a model patient who experienced no relapses and is in full sustained remission. She stated that he is not disabled by alcohol dependency, pathological gambling, or lower-grade depression (dysthymia). She stated petitioner has a good prognosis for continued sobriety even if he experiences significant stressors because he is more stable and has taken an active role in his recovery by participating in . . .[recognized recovery programs] and by developing close friendships with other recovering individuals.[6]

The State Bar's rebuttal witness, Dr. James R. Westphal, an expert in addiction psychiatry, conceded that at the time of his first reinstatement trial, Bellicini's "pathological gambling and alcohol dependency are in sustained full remission and petitioner's dysthymia is in remission. He further reported that petitioner is not currently disabled by his alcohol dependency, pathological gambling or dysthymia."[7]

The hearing judge filed her decision on December 21, 2004, concluding that petitioner had demonstrated by clear and convincing evidence that he was rehabilitated, that he had the requisite ability and learning in the general law, and that he possessed the moral qualifications for reinstatement to the practice of law, which the judge recommended. On review, the hearing judge's reinstatement decision was reversed, even though the review department noted that Bellicini's substantial evidence—in the form of character witnesses, evidence of restitution, and charitable work—all demonstrated petitioner's rehabilitation and good moral character, and supported his reinstatement.

"The hearing judge found 'Petitioner's character witnesses [including members of the "Other Bar" who broke anonymity to testify on behalf of Bellicini] also help demonstrate Petitioner's rehabilitation and good moral character.' We agree."[8] The review department also agreed "with the hearing judge's finding that petitioner's charitable work is a factor supporting his reinstatement," and inserted additional findings in this regard to the record. "Although the hearing judge only noted that petitioner volunteers monthly to discuss with newly-sober patients in recovery how to maintain sobriety, we find that petitioner's work through [a recognized recovery program] in sponsoring a recovering alcoholic and volunteering monthly with [a recognized recovery program's] teleservice also aid his rehabilitative showing."

The review department further stated:

> Unquestionably, we consider evidence of restitution for "its probative value as an indicator of rehabilitation . . . ." The State Bar takes issue with the fact that petitioner waited almost ten years after he resigned before he made restitution and that he made no restitution during the first two years he was in recovery. We do not find that such facts detract from petitioner's showing of rehabilitation, since petitioner continued to suffer from alcoholism for more than eight years after he resigned and was unemployed for approximately one year after

he entered recovery . . . . Therefore, we do not find that the timing of petitioner's restitution detracts from his rehabilitative showing.[9]

Thus, the sole basis of the review department's overturning the first decision on reinstatement was that Bellicini simply had not been sober long enough. Although Bellicini had not been sober for five years at the time he filed his initial petition for reinstatement, he was just two months shy of five years at the time of the review department's reversal order. The review department invited Bellicini to file a subsequent petition one year after the effective date of the opinion.[10]

After some soul-searching, Bellicini decided not to appeal the reversal, despite his feeling that he had been unjustly served. Bellicini resolved instead to stage his comeback via a humble re-filing of the petition, all the while working as a paralegal for his attorney, Jerome Fishkin, former Discipline Prosecutor for the State Bar of California. It was during that time, Bellicini says, that he became certain of his path if reinstatement was indeed granted down the road. He made up his mind that he would work for Fishkin's firm and represent other attorneys in State Bar proceedings.

Bellicini's second petition was granted and the State Bar chose not to appeal. In 2008, nearly 15 years after resigning with charges pending, Bellicini embarked on a successful legal career in which he splits his time between representing attorneys in State Bar proceedings and advising attorneys on ethical matters in order to avoid being summoned into State Bar Court in the first place. He is a frequent speaker on State Bar matters.

Bellicini's comeback has been complete—and inspirational. If your involuntary transition from the practice of law has included discipline, forced resignation or disbarment, it is important to note that it is not impossible to make a case for reinstatement. Of course, the difficulty of the road requires a long look at the reasons *why* you are seeking reinstatement. According to an article by G. M. Filisko in the *ABA Journal*:

> While it's not impossible for a disbarred lawyer to gain reinstatement, the odds are not in the lawyer's favor, and few even try. Data collected for the most recent ABA Survey on Lawyer Disciplinary Systems indicates that 674 petitions, motions or requests for reinstatement

or readmission (which adds retaking the bar exam to other requirements for reinstatement) were filed during 2011 in the jurisdictions
that responded. But only 67 applications for reinstatement after disbarment were successful, according to the survey. (The survey does
not have results from Connecticut, Hawaii and Oklahoma, and has
only partial results from New York.)[11]

Certainly, Bellicini's case demonstrates the diligence and length of time
focused on rehabilitation that must be proven to even pursue this course,
let alone achieve success.[12] As John Gleason, disciplinary counsel and director of regulatory services at the Oregon State Bar, says: "My experience
is that lawyers who are disbarred are generally unhappy with their work
as a lawyer. They've probably found a position they're happy in and have
no interest in coming back." Gleason adds, "It's a fairly low percentage of
lawyers who seek reinstatement."[13]

There are also significant financial considerations. The filing fee in California is about $1,500. Most applicants, like Bellicini, are represented by
counsel, and face lengthy and costly litigation. Filisko reports:

Warren Lupel, special counsel at Much Shelist in Chicago, has represented lawyers and judges in professional responsibility cases for
the past 30 years. His charges range from $20,000 to $25,000. And
he says that amount isn't even the high end for fees in such cases.
"Overall, the reinstatement process is very humbling, almost humili-
ating, and it's onerous and very expensive," Lupel says. "You have to
denude yourself and your family of everything—everybody's health
records, financial records, including every debt you've incurred—and
you go through all that when you're paying the lawyer a substantial
amount of money." It is not, according to the experts, a good idea to
seek reinstatement "just to do it." It is important for lawyers not to
confuse their identity with their law license.[14]

Bellicini agrees that given the difficulties of and expense in pursuing reinstatement, you should seek the reinstatement of your license only if you are

going to use it, not just because it is something you feel you need to check off on your list of making up for the past.

So, what if reinstatement to the practice of law is not your next step? What if your comeback is meant to be in another field altogether?

Good news. Chapter 6 is for you. You now find yourself squarely in the camp of formerly practicing attorneys who are seeking alternate employment, and there are many resources available to you. Importantly, every single one of the attorneys whom I have spoken to who has transitioned from the practice of law to an alternative career altogether has conceded that their law degree and prior legal training differentiated them from the pack in succeeding in their second (or third! Or fourth!) career.

Consider world-famous jewelry designer Jill Donovan, whose designs are coveted by celebrities including Harry Connick, Jr., Miranda Lambert, and *New York Times* best-selling author (and transitioning attorney in her own right) Emily Giffin. Donovan says that her former legal career makes her a shrewd negotiator and is an instant legitimizer in business meetings that have grown her business, in just three years, to one in which her payroll alone exceeds her highest legal salary.

Consider also Nathan Sawaya, world-famous Lego brick artist, who admits that even though he never really wanted to practice law, his legal background allowed him to negotiate early art contracts and deals that helped separate him in a world of talented artists all vying for attention in the New York City art world. When we spoke in the spring of 2014, Sawaya had just wrapped up a job creating designs for Lady Gaga's most recent music video, and was on his way to open a new exhibit in Dublin.

In short, whether or not you seek to be reinstated to the practice of law, or even if attempts are unsuccessful, your prior legal training can still be the catalyst for renewal.

And then—when you are ready—it is never too late to stage your Second Act.

## Notes

1. *In re Samuel L. Bellicini*, 03-R-03728, J. Watai (Review Dep't of the State Bar Ct., filed March 6, 2006), at 1, http://www.statebarcourt.ca.gov/portals/2/documents /opinions/Bellicini.pdf.

2. *Id.* at 7.

3. *Id.* at 6.

4. *Id.* at 7.

5. *In re Samuel Bellicini*, State Bar No. 152191, No. 93 CV 03942 MISC VRW (Order of Reinstatement filed January 26, 2009, effective date October 10, 2008), https://cases.justia.com/federal/district-courts/california/candce/3:1993cv03942 /86504/5/0.pdf?ts=1377049373.

6. *In re Samuel L. Bellicini*, 03-R-03728, J. Watai (Review Dep't of the State Bar Ct., filed March 6, 2006), at 9-10, http://www.statebarcourt.ca.gov/portals/2/ documents/opinions/Bellicini.pdf.

7. *Id.* at 10.

8. *Id.* at 12.

9. *Id.* at 16.

10. *Id.* at 23.

11. G. M. Filisko, *Disbarred Lawyers Who Seek Reinstatement Have a Rough Road to Redemption*, A.B.A. J. (August 1, 2013), http://www.abajournal.com/ magazine/article/disbarred_lawyers_who_seek_reinstatement_have_a_rough_road _to_redemption.

12. *Id.*

13. *Id.*

14. *Id.*

## Chapter 5

# Leaving a Law Firm for an Alternate Legal Career

*In my opinion, the law school experience has really moved away from its origins and has instead become focused on teaching people how to be employees. . . . I had been teaching a class at the law school for a while on alternatives to the traditional employee model, when one day one of my students came running out of class, following alongside of me, asking: "Do they know? Do they know what you're actually teaching in this class?" I laughed, and said: "I'm pretty sure they don't." He said: "Well, if they did, they'd never have let you out of your cage!"*
—Susan Cartier Liebel, founder of Solo Practice University

It is undeniable that the law school model has, in recent history, focused its training on preparing its graduates to be employees. Whereas the earliest law school experience was focused on apprenticeship, creating a vehicle for independent practice, it is undisputed that law schools have abandoned the apprenticeship model. Instead, law firms have been vying to place graduates as employees at the most prestigious law firms, and have been touting those placement statistics as a key component of their recruitment of new students. Law schools, to put it simply, have long been competing with each other to create the most and the "best" employees.

While the climate is shifting slowly—very, very slowly—due to the economic constraints leading law firms to hire *fewer* employees each year, the career counseling programs at many top law schools are still very much focused on traditional avenues for their graduates and alums, even though alumni are actively seeking alternatives. National Association for Law Placement (NALP) statistics confirm that in the past several years, the percentage of law grads starting their careers in the business arena has more than doubled since the 1990s, from 8 percent to 18 percent. According to the "Employment Report and Salary Survey for the Class of 2012" released by the NALP, the employment rate for new law school graduates fell for the fifth straight year in a row since 2008—from 85.6 percent (2011) to 84.7 percent in 2012.[1] Yet, the law school career counselors I spoke to while writing this book, such as Jill Backer, the newest associate dean for the Career Development Office at Pace Law School, readily concede that due to reporting requirements and hiring statistics, they are often constrained to focus career counseling for law graduates—and even alumni—on "JD-required" positions.

Caroll Welch, a career coach and counselor and former practicing attorney, has had the chance to work at both the Pace Law School Career Outreach Office and then at New Directions for Attorneys. She admits that it was "liberating" to go from traditional law school placement to New Directions, a career re-entry program specifically geared to attorneys, which she called a "much more three-dimensional job."

Liz Brown, former litigation partner, frequent speaker on alternative career choices, and author of the acclaimed book *Life After Law*, recounts her experience when she wanted to leave big law in about 2009. She visited the alumni career office at her alma mater, Harvard Law School, to see what alternatives they could offer. "No problem," they said. "How about a position in-house? How about government?"

More traditional positions. More employee positions.

After all, what else could there be for a smart, highly creative, experienced, Harvard-trained lawyer?

How about: *much more*?

Remember when you graduated from law school, and not one single person asked if you wanted to go to law school forever, or go back there? What if—when and if you wished to—you could also *graduate* from being a law firm employee? Into an alternative legal career?

The truth is, the hardest part is not going to be getting an alternative legal career. The hardest part is going to be figuring out what alternative careers are even out there for formerly practicing attorneys, and navigating the questions from colleagues, family, and friends who are still likely to ask when you are going back to the traditional practice of law. Which is why I've included Chapter 8 (Dealing with Fallout).

So. Where to find these alternative careers for lawyers? And how to successfully transition to one?

1. Prepare yourself to graduate
2. Consider an alternative way to practice law
3. Look into informational interviewing made easy
4. Consider what it is you would do for free

## Prepare Yourself to Graduate

Since working on this book, I have asked every single transitioning lawyer I come into contact with one common question: "If you were at a cocktail party, and someone were to come over and ask if you are a lawyer, what would you say?"

Nearly everyone trips over that answer.

"Um, I was a lawyer, but now I'm not."

"I don't practice anymore, but I used to be a lawyer. Well, I still have my license—I just don't—"

"Uh, hmm. Good question."

My own answer used to be: "Well, I *was* a lawyer. In a past life." Which is a horrible answer, of course.

Debra Vey Voda-Hamilton, founder of Hamilton Law and Mediation, gave me the most shocking answer of all. Voda-Hamilton says that during her hiatus from practicing law, "I never ever told people I was a lawyer. I didn't feel I could say such a thing given that I was no longer practicing." She told me that when she started practicing again after a 13-year hiatus, her own friends and neighbors were flabbergasted to learn that she was, in fact, a lawyer.

After a 13-year career as a litigator, and a subsequent 13-year hiatus, Voda-Hamilton has indeed "graduated" into a new legal career altogether. Founder of Hamilton Law and Mediation—a firm that does 0 percent litigation and 100 percent mediation—Voda-Hamilton is admitted to practice law in all New York State courts, but focuses her career exclusively on mediation, speaking, and writing.

Voda-Hamilton was a speaker at the 2013 American Veterinary Medical Law Association, discussing how employing alternative dispute resolution methodology in animal law conflicts may expedite resolution of veterinary malpractice and other client conflicts without the need for litigation. She has spoken at several veterinary schools and conferences, the American Kennel Club, the Human Animal Bond Organization, state bar association animal law committees, and animal interest groups, outlining the value of using alternative dispute resolution in solving their own conflicts. Voda-Hamilton also writes a monthly blog for Hamilton Law and Mediation and is a monthly contributor to Solo Practice University and *Canine Chronicle*.[2]

Voda-Hamilton admits that family members often still ask her when she is planning to return to litigation, and that she has struggled over the years to answer her own version of the "Are you a lawyer?" question.

In contrast, Erin Giglia, co-founder of the innovative Montage Legal Group, a company that pairs freelance high-credentialed attorneys with firms requiring specialized project work, rarely practices law herself, yet answers my question "Do you still tell people you are a lawyer?" with an emphatic "Yes, of course!" Giglia insists that she rarely fields questions about whether she is going to "return" to the practice of law she left in 2009. Giglia says "when you have a business, when you are a successful entrepreneur . . . no one asks you if you intend to go back to the life you had before." They understand in some sense that she has graduated, and Giglia's ability to embrace that fact too has no doubt aided in the transition.

The bottom line is that I have learned from my research that the majority of hurdles for transitioning attorneys can be boiled down to two very manageable categories: identity issues and financial issues. In Chapter 3, we discussed the very real financial considerations, with advice that really could be heeded by any transitioning attorney, whether or not becoming a full-time unpaid caregiver.

As for identity issues: Though these can be, in many ways, even more crippling than the financial issues that may accompany transitioning from the practice of law, they also can be answered much more simply than the financial considerations at play.

Say it with me:

"I am a lawyer. I am still a lawyer. I will always be a lawyer."

When you are about to willingly graduate from being a law firm employee or even from the practice of law altogether, or if you have already transitioned, work on your answer to that cocktail-party question.

Say it out loud. And then move on.

## Consider an Alternative Way to Practice Law

In her acclaimed book, *Life After Law*, Liz Brown offers profiles of attorneys who have sought a variety of fulfilling and unique positions—never dismissing their legal training, but rather embracing the versatility of it.

Attorneys like Meredith Benedict, who left her big law firm job to start a new development job at Boston Medical Center. "Her new boss saw her J.D. as an asset. He was married to a lawyer who started her own nonprofit, and understood that lawyers who changed careers brought terrific skills to the table . . . . [H]er legal training helped her see the big picture strategic goals while staying focused on all the detailed steps needed to reach those goals. Eventually, she became the director of her group."[3]

Add to Liz Brown's list attorneys like Kim Yonta, who, after more than a decade of working as an assistant prosecutor, transitioned to a solo practitioner, opening her own law firm. "How did you know how to do such a thing?" I asked Yonta when we spoke in 2014. She agreed that law school did not prepare her to be a small business owner, even though that is exactly what she is now. "I have to set aside time every weekend to work on billing and administration issues." Importantly, Yonta consulted with a small business consultant prior to opening the firm, and advises every would-be solo practitioner to do the same.

Former practicing attorney Susan Cartier Liebel actually transitioned from the practice of law to start a cottage industry for lawyers who want to hang out their own shingle. Liebel points out that the possibility of solo practice is not just overlooked in law school. Solo practice as a career path, Liebel claims, is actually discouraged—rather than encouraged—in law school. "The law school environment does not support or value the decision to open one's own practice," Liebel told me when we spoke in the summer of 2014. So, in 2009, Liebel started Solo Practice University, an independent virtual program for lawyers who want to learn how to start their own business and practice on their own.

Liebel came to law school from a business and entrepreneurial background, having worked as a recruiter and in the advertising industry for 10 years. She loved the idea that when you graduate from law school, you have the opportunity to be "the product" you go out into the world to market, but she quickly realized that in law school, the current culture does not encourage the idea of going out on your own. Liebel says, "You are trained to be an employee, which actually diminishes the value of the education." So, Liebel set out to navigate law school to get the most out of her degree—and to learn how to start her own practice afterward.

After graduating from law school, she opened her own law firm with two other colleagues. She succeeded in cases against much bigger firms, a fact she attributes to her love of blending creativity with the practice of law. She credits her successes to avoiding the "employee" mentality and attacking her cases with the ingenuity and outside-the-box thinking that developed from running her own firm. She also taught on the side at her own law school alma mater—a class that she claims targeted those "underground students" who wanted to learn entrepreneurial skills.

She did not stay underground for long. In fact, after eight years of teaching the class, she was asked to convert her class to a non-credit course. It turned out that too many people wanted to take her class, and the law school claimed that it could not comfortably accommodate all the students who were seeking out Liebel's unique brand of entrepreneurial training. Liebel realized at this juncture that things were in place for a full-time transition from her own practice of law. So, when a former student contacted her around that time to say that he would love to help build websites for her graduating students who went into solo practice, Liebel responded simply, "No. I have a much bigger idea."

Solo Practice University was born.

Liebel argues that although it may be hard to believe, given all the statistics and anecdotes about noncreative, depressed lawyers, law school does not actually attract noncreative, depressed people. In fact, Liebel claims, law school attracts many happy, creative people and then gives them no outlet for that creativity.

"So, it would seem that some people who think they hate practicing law, don't actually hate practicing law—they hate the *way* they are practicing law?" I asked Liebel.

"Exactly," she agreed.

If you don't believe Liebel's theory about the inherent creativity of lawyers, don't tell Anna Palmer, who co-founded the Boston-based Fashion Project with a law school classmate immediately after graduation. The business collects posh apparel and accessories and then sells the tax-deductible gifts on behalf of charities like Dress for Success and the March of Dimes. If you still don't believe Liebel's theory about the inherent creativity of lawyers, certainly do not tell Genavieve Shingle.

Genavieve Shingle spent 1½ years in Manhattan as a corporate M&A attorney before she decided that law firm life was not for her. She started her own business catering to entrepreneurs, focusing on the problems and documents and issues that are unique to entrepreneurs, and in 2014 started a profitable business on the same day she publicly announced her last day as a law firm employee. Shingle started a business called "Lawyer in Your Pocket," renamed (due to trademark issues) a few months later to—wait for it—"Damsel in Defense."

Who says lawyers lack creativity?

Within nine months, Shingle's earnings had surpassed six figures (although she readily conceded that her start-up expenses had been almost equally high.)

What's her secret?

"Simple," says Shingle. "I'm not self-conscious." Shingle is not afraid to network, to pitch herself, or to approach high-level executives. She believes in her model, believes in her value, and has the happy clients to show for that confidence. She has financed her endeavor herself, refusing to take on an investor, although she has hired a PR coach, and has a mentor to advise her on the ethical issues rife in the new arena in which she practices. Shingle markets her services to a niche of like-minded entrepreneurs tired of the old way of hiring attorneys and anxious for a creative outlook that matches their own business models.

New times call for new lawyers.

Nowhere is that more evident than with the rise of the virtual firm. Many attorneys today have alternatives to the traditional ways of practicing law that do not involve being an employee, but rather an independent contractor—emphasis on the word *independent*.

One great example of this new trend in legal representation is Montage Legal Group, a company that organizes and markets highly credentialed freelance attorneys to small and large firms for project work. Montage Legal Group—founded by two mom lawyer friends, Erin Giglia and Laurie Gormican Rowen, who transitioned from litigation to caregiving in 2009—staffs project legal work for firms of all sizes. Montage Legal Group recruits a pool of highly credentialed lawyers who graduated from the top law schools, with practice experience from the country's top law firms, who just so happen to be largely women who have left the practice of law to become full-time caregivers to children—a sizeable pool of untapped resources.

Until now.

Of course, to say that Montage Legal Group "recruits" this highly qualified candidate pool may not be wholly accurate. As co-founder Erin Giglia admits, admission to the Montage Legal Group is not granted to every one of the more than 1,000 applicants who knock on Montage Legal Group's door. Indeed, that the group can be so selective is highly indicative of the quality of attorneys out there who no longer practice in a traditional way but who want to be practicing in some way. A different way.

When we spoke in the fall of 2014, I asked Giglia about how and where she advertises for freelance attorneys. She says that in the history of the company, they have *never* had to advertise, something she admits is a "telling sign" about the state of the litigation practice today, especially for women.

"Freelance attorneys have been around forever," says Giglia. "But we've organized it. We've made it easier for high-quality attorneys and law firms needing their services to find each other." A service that was obviously needed! Little marketing and a small initial budget were required to get the idea off the ground, as the women admit that in 2010 they each invested just $2,000 to start the company.[4]

In 2014, Giglia told me she has more than 200 attorneys in the database, and Montage Legal Group has worked with hundreds of firms of all sizes. At least 90 percent of their firm clients are repeat clients, a very significant statistic. In 2013, Montage made just over $1 million in revenue and in 2014, they were expecting to exceed that figure, according to Giglia.[5]

Indeed, the freelance attorney biz is not just profitable for those organizing it, like Giglia. Freelance attorney work is quite possibly the most lucrative part-time gig out there. According to PayScale.com, "Attorney/ Lawyer" is the top-paying job for part-time, self-employed workers, with a median hourly pay of $147.40.[6]

Still not convinced that alternative, virtual, or solo practice is for you? Not to worry. There are choices. Lots of choices. And just as many ways to find them.

## Look into Informational Interviewing Made Easy

Marc Luber is perhaps the quintessential informational interviewer. Always a firm believer that he would do with his law degree something other than become an employee of a law firm, Luber has now created an award-winning video website that seeks to show lawyers the other available careers out there. So it is—no surprise—called JDCareersOutThere.com (JDCOT for short).

After a storied post-law school career that included going on the road with the Rolling Stones and becoming a record executive and band manager, Luber became a legal headhunter for a decade. It was during that time that Luber says he first remembers seeing scores of people who hated being practicing lawyers. He wished he could help them but he couldn't. After all, he had clients to help. Clients who wanted to hire people who wanted to be lawyers.

While a headhunter, Luber recounts that he was always asking people about their careers. One day, he was interviewing a cellist at a restaurant dinner party about his profession, when someone at the table said, "You should really have your own talk show interviewing people about their careers." Luber says that right then and there, he wrote down "talk show" and "interview people about their careers"on a restaurant napkin.

In 2010, Luber first started with a broader mission: Careers Out There. But in 2013, he started focusing on those attorneys he remembered from his legal recruiting days: attorneys who hated practicing law. His video website was nominated in 2013 for ABA Journal Law Blawg 100 for top law blogs, and voted "Best Law Career Site" by a reader poll. Luber says his award-winning site is meant to do what law schools do not: namely, educate lawyers about potential legal careers—all of them.

Essentially a vehicle for informational interviewing made easy, Luber interviews attorneys in a wide variety of fields and asks questions—lots of questions. As Luber says, "There are jobs out there people don't even know exist." He makes it his business to bring those jobs out from the underground.

Shedding light on little-known JD career paths such as advocacy careers (interview with Abby Leibman, President and CEO of Mazon, A Jewish Response to Hunger, http://jdcareersoutthere.com/social-justice-advocacy-careers-with-abby-leibman) and legal knowledge management (interview with David Hobbie, Litigation Knowledge Manager for Goodwin Procter, http://jdcareersoutthere.com/what-is-legal-knowledge-management-an-a lternative-career-for-lawyers-at-a-law-firm), Luber elicits practical information from his interviewees that includes financial considerations and day-to-day responsibilities.

Liz Brown's *Life After Law* and accompanying blog (http://lizbrownjd .com) are wonderful and practical resources for would-be transitioning attorneys. By illustrating eight career paths for formerly practicing attorneys (including writing, entrepreneurial, and consulting paths), *Life After Law* gives real-life examples of attorneys who have shifted from the active practice of law using the JD they have learned to love and appreciate.[7]

And just when you start to think that maybe there are too many choices—too many alternatives available to an attorney who wants to graduate from the practice of law or from being a law firm employee—you can whittle down your choices with one simple question: What would you do for free?

## Consider What It Is You Would Do for Free

Casey Berman (University of California, Hastings '99) is a technology executive, and former market research consultant, investment banker, and in-house counsel based in San Francisco. He is also the founder of "Leave Law Behind," a blog and community that focuses on helping unhappy attorneys leave the law.

Berman, like many other experts in the field of recruitment and professional transitions, espouses self-analysis. He has distilled self-analysis for lawyers into three impactful, actionable questions:

1. For what type of advice do people come to you?
2. What do people compliment you on?

And perhaps my favorite:

3. What are you already doing (or would you do) for free to help people?[8]

Deborah Epstein Henry, best-selling author of *Law & Reorder: Legal Industry Solutions for Restructure, Retention, Promotion & Work/Life Balance* (ABA, 2010), and frequent speaker to audiences of active and formerly practicing attorneys, agrees. To an extent.

Epstein Henry, a former practicing litigator, is an internationally recognized expert and consultant on the future of the profession, new legal models, women's issues, and work-life balance. Epstein Henry is president of Flex-Time Lawyers LLC, an international consulting firm she founded in the late 1990s. Her firm is well known for running "Best Law Firms for Women" with *Working Mother* magazine—a national survey conducted since 2007 to select the top 50 law firms for women and report on industry trends. She is also co-founder and managing director of Bliss Lawyers, a secondment firm placing high-caliber lawyers in positions on a temporary basis with in-house legal departments and law firms; at times, these placements convert into permanent employment.

As Epstein Henry points out, if and when you decide it is time to graduate from the practice of law, it can be a wonderful time to explore the things you are interested in. Participate in nonprofits (not just the kids' school), engage in volunteer work, trade association, and nonprofit work for the bar. Explore your real interests. For example, consider what you are reading purely for fun. But, as Epstein Henry points out, it is not enough to stop at the "what would I do for free" question.

"You might love knitting, but you might be terrible at it. Or you might love knitting and be really good at it, but no one, let's say, buys knitted sweaters anymore. The point is to assess not only your interests, but also your strengths and the market needs." In other words, in making the transition from the practice of law to an alternative career, you need to consider the point where your passions, strengths, and market needs all intersect.

Put another way, you should decide what you *would* do for free.

That you do not *have* to do for free.

## Notes

1. Hollee Schwartz Temple, *Law Students Prepare for Jobs Outside Firms*, A.B.A. J. (December 1, 2013), http://www.abajournal.com/magazine/article/law_students _prepare_for_jobs_outside_firms.

2. http://hamiltonlawandmediation.blogspot.com.

3. Liz Brown, J.D., *Life After Law* (Massachusetts: Bibliomotion, 2013), at 122.

4. Mamie Joeveer, *How Two Stay-at-Home-Moms Are Changing the Legal Industry*, Forbes.com (August 27, 2014).

5. *Id.*

6. Kimberly Palmer, *The Best-Paid Moonlighting Jobs in America*, News & World Rep. (August 23, 2012), http://money.usnews.com/money/blogs/alpha-consumer /2012/08/23/the-best-paid-moonlighting-jobs-in-america.

7. Liz Brown, J.D., *Life After Law* (Massachusetts: Bibliomotion, 2013).

8. Casey Berman, The Third Step in Leaving Law Behind—Do What You Are Good At, AboveTheLaw.com (March 28, 2013), http://abovethelaw.com/career-files /the-third-step-in-leaving-law-behind-do-what-you-are-good-at.

# Chapter 6

# Leaving the Law for a Second (or Third!) Career

*Years ago, I decided to focus on mastering one skill per year. I wanted at the end of my life to have not just one thing I was really good at, but over 30 things that I could say I had done well. One year, I learned Russian, and even spent 8 weeks at the end of the year, traveling to the country, immersing myself in the language. I took up running, learned how to play poker, and learned to tap dance . . . . One year, I took up jewelry design, and that was just something I had a "craving" for, something I always wanted to go back to. Eventually.*

—Jill Donovan, celebrity jewelry designer, founder of Rustic Cuff, and former practicing attorney and law professor.

Every year, I am invited to Taylor Swift's high school alma mater to give a talk on career day. I am the designated lawyer for the day, even though I no longer practice law for a living. Most likely it's because I am the only lawyer in the area who has enough flexibility in her schedule to actually take the morning off.

I tell the students the same thing every year. "A law degree is a heck of a lot more versatile than a guitar and a ticket to Nashville." That is not to say that a law career is one to pursue if you do not know what else to do. I make that point very clear to the students every year. There is substantial evidence that treating the law as a default career path has very likely led to the increasing numbers of disgruntled lawyers. "People still go to law school for the wrong reasons," says Art Bousel, career coach and owner of the Lawyer Career Spa, an innovative place he calls a "haven for complete immersion in career transformation."

Let me make something clear if I have not done so already. I love being a lawyer. I have used my law degree to work at one of the top law firms in the country. It has been my tool to negotiate multimillion-dollar deals, and to argue motions in state and federal courts in several states across the country. My law degree has been an unquestionable asset as I have worked to help run a start-up company that raised money for numerous grassroots and large charities and helped to grow the businesses of more than 100 artisan designers. I have also relied upon my law degree to negotiate two publishing deals (and counting!). But in 2009, when I first started to think about doing something other than practice law with my law degree, I felt somewhat lost.

Essentially, as many have pointed out, despite some advancements in recent years, law firms still operate as one of the last legal pyramid schemes in our business world. The billable-hour model, though criticized and challenged by many clients in the post-Lehman fallout era, still remains the prevalent model in law firms. Thus, the top tier of equity partners requires huge numbers of lower-level associates to feed the top. Because law schools still focus their career counseling and job recruiting primarily on law firms (especially big law firms), many lawyers leave law school with little information about alternative careers. And because few lawyers—other than Rustic Cuff founder, Jill Donovan, that is—proactively undertake to hone a skill or hobby each year, few lawyers know what they are good at other than practicing law until they actually leave.

"Lawyers are, by nature, risk averse," Nathan Sawaya (corporate lawyer turned world-famous Lego brick artist) pointed out when we spoke in the spring of 2014. Sawaya left the world of corporate law in 2004 to become a commercial artist, a move he says was supported by family and friends, although it left his lawyer friends and colleagues "confused." In March 2014, Sawaya had just wrapped up work on a video for pop musician Lady Gaga, and his "The Art of the Brick" exhibit was an unqualified success, having shown in more than 25 cities in North America, Australia, Asia, and Europe.[1] He took a risk leaving the practice of law—one that paid off in spades. But how to take that first step? That first risk?

It is difficult for lawyers—even unsatisfied, unfulfilled lawyers—to leave the practice of law for alternative careers. Moreover, it is hard to find the moral support from your lawyer friends and colleagues to leave law for an alternative career. Let's face it. They too are risk averse.

Yet, if you are one of the lawyers who has, as law-partner-turned-business-law professor and author Liz Brown puts it, "that gnawing feeling in their stomachs as they approach the office every day and as they check their e-mail at night,"[2] it may be time to ask yourself why you are not using the most versatile asset you own to get out. In *Life After Law*, Brown reports that "to this day, I have not met a single former lawyer who regrets changing professions. Most wish they had done it sooner."[3]

So, how can you overcome your risk-averse tendencies?

I am glad you asked. It is fairly simple, actually.

1. Say it out loud
2. Make a paradigm shift that does not shed your lawyer identity
3. Do it on the side
4. Wait for your website to crash

## Say It Out Loud

Lawyers—disgruntled ones, anyway—are infamous for griping about what they do not like about practicing law. But they are not always as good at vocalizing things they are actually interested in and enthusiastic about.

In *Life After Law*, Liz Brown advises lawyers exploring alternative careers to write down things that interest them. She also suggests career coaching and reaching out to people with interesting jobs for informational interviews. All of this is really a more detailed program of "saying it out loud."

As Marc Luber, founder of the award-winning video website JDCareersOutThere.com, advises, the simple act of articulating to someone, "What you do for a living sounds interesting. I'd love to hear more about it," can be a great first step to investigating alternative careers outside of the law. Brown, a frequent speaker on alternative law careers, concurs. "When someone's work sounded interesting to me, I asked her out for coffee. The kindness of strangers amazed me. I had no idea how generous people were until I got out of law firms."[4]

You should also be sure to say it out loud at cocktail parties, to friends over lunch, and even on social media. Rustic Cuff's Jill Donovan tells the story of the moment she decided to make her jewelry hobby a sustainable career. She said out loud to one friend: "I sold $20,000 worth of jewelry this year. I want to sell $100,000 worth of jewelry next year." She said it, wrote it down, and wouldn't you know it? She met and surpassed her goal the following year. There were home jewelry shows and loyal support of friends, repeat customers, and hard, hard work that helped make the dream a reality. But it all started with one single statement.

Uttered out loud.

## Make a Paradigm Shift That Does Not Shed Your Lawyer Identity

When I talk to reformed practicing lawyers, I find that one of the biggest issues is how to define yourself after leaving the practice of law. I too have found myself stumbling over these words: "I'm a lawyer. Well, I was a lawyer. Well, in my past life, I was a lawyer, but now I'm a—"

A what?

Guess what. I'm still a lawyer.

*And you will be too.*

Several years into my sabbatical, I had been working with a wonderful start-up company that was evolving and making a new brand iteration. I was contemplating my role in the new brand when the attorney from the investor called me to discuss that very issue. I had come to see him as "the lawyer" in our relationship. I was posturing to become the new vice president of the brand, and I was no longer practicing law in my new position.

Nevertheless, as we discussed my future, the issue of my requested salary increase came up, and I told him that I was going to request what was essentially a 50 percent pay increase to bring my salary in line with what I felt the company could afford and my position should pay. Mind you, the numbers we were talking about were still a fraction—perhaps a third or a quarter—of my former full-time law firm salary.

We danced back and forth on the issue for quite a while, the company attorney relying heavily on the "this company is still in start-up phase right now" argument, until finally, I asked this question: "Do you think that what I am asking for is a reasonable salary?"

He agreed that it was.

"And one of my primary responsibilities is going to be to negotiate with outside vendors, right?"

He agreed again.

"Then how can you trust me to negotiate with any outside parties if I cannot even negotiate what you have conceded would be a reasonable salary for myself?"

I became vice president, with the requested salary increase, effective immediately.

I also realized that I was still—and ever would be—a lawyer. Even without the corporate litigator title I had left behind.

Susan Packard, a founding executive behind CNBC, HGTV, Food Network, and others, writes about leaving a senior corporate role—not a legal position, but the idea is translatable—as she concedes that "it is indeed a process to shed all the corporate armor and to quiet our ego."[5] She also points out that there is some evidence "that retired male CEO's have the greatest incidence of heart attacks on Mondays,"[6] giving credence to the notion that shedding one's ingrained professional identity can have serious and even devastating consequences.

Art Bousel is a former practicing attorney, and now career coach/entrepreneur and founder of the Lawyer Career Spa in Portland Oregon, a place he describes as a "haven for complete immersion in career transformation." Bousel recalls a pivotal moment from his 1990s transition from practicing attorney to entrepreneur, in which he had recently founded a food marketing company. He had scored a big meeting with a supermarket executive and went into the meeting elated about finally making the transition away from lawyer. Suddenly, Bousel recalls, "I was so nervous, I couldn't say a word." The executive spoke up, telling Bousel that he believed wholeheartedly in

Bousel's model and concept, especially "given that you are an attorney." Bousel laughed and realized instantly that though he was leaving behind a career practicing law, he was not leaving behind his lawyer identity, and that was a very positive realization.

The truth is, unlike the "job title" you may leave behind, you need not leave behind your lawyer identity if you seek out an alternative career. For good or for bad, you can still be a lawyer even if you decide to leave the active practice of law voluntarily. Three years of study, a degree, and bar membership(s) do not need to vanish into thin air when you stop practicing law.

Indeed, this axiom is why I was not really surprised to hear Jill Donovan tell me that she still tells strangers who ask what she does for a living, *first,* that she is a lawyer and a law professor. This is a woman who now owns a thriving jewelry design business, Rustic Cuff. Her designs have been featured in prominent national publications, including *Elle, O Magazine, People,* and *Women's World Magazine.* Her jewelry has been worn by mega-celebrities, including Miranda Lambert, Harry Connick, Jr., Kathie Lee Gifford, Sheryl Crow, and Guiliana Rancic, just to name a few.[7] Nevertheless, Donovan admits that she still identifies herself as a lawyer. "There is a quantifiable assumption that goes with" being a lawyer. Instead of having to explain to a stranger that her jewelry business is indeed hugely and objectively successful, that she has 15 employees, and that her payroll alone is more than she ever made practicing law, Donovan says it is easier to gain respect by just saying the words: "I am a lawyer." The author of *Life After Law,* Liz Brown, agrees. "Law is still a generally respected profession, lawyer jokes notwithstanding."[8]

Moreover, as the transitioning attorneys I spoke with agree—without exception—your law degree, no matter what alternative career you eventually choose, will still likely be one of the biggest assets you bring to the table in navigating your alternative career path. Nathan Sawaya admits that he never really wanted to be a practicing lawyer, but after college he did not have enough faith in his art as a viable career, so he took the natural path for all aspiring artists at the end of college: "I went to law school." Nevertheless, Sawaya is quick to acknowledge that his law degree has given him an edge that other aspiring artists might not have. The ability to negotiate, and to do so quickly, as deals in the art world are often time sensitive, has been an admittedly key factor in his post-law success. Sawaya was able to negotiate early deals on his own without losing valuable time or resources, and without having to hunt down an attorney to do so for him.

Jill Donovan agrees that her law degree has provided the credibility necessary to help her business grow. "I really don't think I'd be here without it. Maybe the ultimate customer doesn't care that I have a law degree, but in the business and financial world, in meetings with retailers and banks—it matters. It really does."

Put simply, there is no need to regret, second-guess, or (conversely) grasp onto the time you spent as a practicing lawyer. As you "quiet" that role to explore an alternative career, there is certainly no need to stop identifying yourself as a lawyer. Once you respect your law degree and former law career as an invaluable asset you take with you into your next career step, you will stop stumbling over how to describe yourself to others.

And to yourself.

## Do It on the Side

Unless you are independently wealthy or do not have to work, you may have to be prepared to pursue your alternative career on the side for a while. Nathan Sawaya worked on art six hours per night—every night—after he came home from his Manhattan law firm job for several years before he transitioned to professional artist. In the initial years of Rustic Cuff, Jill Donovan worked on her jewelry business while still maintaining her license and professor position at the University of Tulsa.

If you want an alternative career, you too may have to do it "on the side," a phrase that can be interpreted literally or figuratively. Literally, you can do what Nathan Sawaya did. Cultivate your second career at night after finishing your day at the law firm, until your second career is an economically viable primary career.

Figuratively, "doing it on the side" might take the form of "dressing like a lawyer" for a while, as *Back on the Career Track* co-author Carol Cohen puts it. Keep up all licenses and meet all outstanding CLE requirements.

Keep your subscriptions to relevant legal journals and continue to keep bridges and doors open to your past while you explore an alternative career to practicing law in your future. Seek out informational interviews about professions that interest you while you still hold yourself out as a "lawyer."

Check out the career alternatives described in Liz Brown's *Life After Law*, and on her site: www. http://lizbrownjd.com. Casey Berman, a frequent speaker and consultant on alternative legal careers, has another great resource in his blog: http://leavelawbehind.com. "Virtual" informational interviewing is available on Mark Luber's award-winning JDCareersOut-There.com video website.

And don't be afraid to change direction. Even at the last minute. Harvard-trained business law professor and former litigator Liz Brown describes how, when she first thought about leaving her law firm partnership position, she set about going into development (fundraising). She took a class, did numerous informational interviews, and researched the field extensively, until she eventually realized it was not for her. She had to acknowledge, after taking all of the steps necessary to embark on her new career path, that she did not actually like asking people for money.[9] "It was embarrassing to go back to the drawing board, but better than committing to another unfulfilling job."[10] Brown also gives prophetic advice to would-be alternative career launchers: "[Y]ou don't need to know where you are going to end up at the right place . . . every step led me to the next one, but I couldn't see the whole path at any point in the process."[11]

In addition to cultivating informational interviews and your networking field, you will have to cultivate patience. Depending on how you define success in your alternative career, success may take some time. If you want to leave the practice of law to become a barista, so be it. Embrace and enjoy. But if you want to leave the practice of law to run your own coffee shop, realize that it will not happen overnight and you will need to be prepared for that.

But here is the good news about all the hard work that seeking out and succeeding in an alternative career is going to entail: You are a lawyer. You're good at that.

After I left big law, working for a virtual start-up company with team members in the Philippines, out west, down south, and in New York City meant the same kind of 24-hour-a-day availability I had when I was working on legal briefs in my Skadden Arps Times Square office building for a living. But I assure you that I was prepared for that life by those days and nights in Times Square, and I am grateful for that experience. Professional and personal fulfillment do not necessarily happen between the hours of 9 and 5, and that will not change just because you want to stop practicing law.

Art Bousel, career coach and founder of the innovative Lawyer Career Spa, known as "a haven for complete immersion in career transformation, away from daily distractions," notes that lifestyle is not the only consideration in lawyer happiness and fulfillment. Bousel says that the happiest lawyers are those closest in the chain of commerce to the client. "In my experience, those who are most unhappy are those farthest removed from a client who is doing anything." This is definitely wise advice to keep in mind as you explore alternative careers.

After you have explored alternative careers, cultivated an alternative career on the side, and shifted (but not eliminated) your way of thinking about yourself as a lawyer, you may naturally overcome your risk-averse nature. But if not, there is another step you can take.

Or perhaps more accurately, wait for.

## Wait for Your Website to Crash

Nathan Sawaya was arguably ahead of his time in 2003 and 2004. At a time when "web logs" or "blogs" were brand new, particularly in the art industry, he set up an art blog, showing off the creations he was making at night after long hours at his Manhattan corporate law firm. He was receiving website hits, and some professional commissions, but one day in 2004, when his website crashed from so many hits, he began to think that maybe there was enough interest in his art to pursue it as a viable career. He left his corporate law career at Winston & Strawn soon after and never looked back.

Rustic Cuff founder Jill Donovan describes the moment her "website crashed." After showing some of her jewelry creations to a friend, the friend begged for the opportunity to host an event in her home to show off Donovan's unique creations to other friends. After Donovan reluctantly agreed,

100 guests arrived, and nearly every one ordered one or two cuffs. Donovan sold $10,000 worth of jewelry that night and spent the next four months finishing jewelry and fulfilling orders she had never anticipated. Soon thereafter she started working on the brand full time, treating it as much more than an on-the-side "hobby."

There are other less dramatic examples of crashing websites, of course. Former Judge Todd Singer was able to pursue his long-held dream of teaching an underserved population, after his children were nearly done with college and family financial considerations had changed significantly.

Caroll Welch, who relaunched her legal career in 2012 by joining the administration of Pace Law School, and later becoming assistant director of the New Directions for Attorneys program, enrolled in a certificate program at NYU in coaching, and with New Directions's blessing started seeing private clients on the side: coaching disgruntled lawyers about possible transitions. Eventually she was able to leave New Directions in 2014 to work with private clients full time.

Art Bousel, founder of Lawyer Career Spa, has been coaching unsatisfied attorneys since the 1990s. A business article that featured Bousel's personal story of lawyer-turned-entrepreneur ran in the mid-1990s in *Crain's Chicago Business,* and it sparked a host of unsolicited calls to Bousel from disgruntled attorneys who wanted to know how Bousel had made the transition they were longing to make.[12] Bousel began coaching these attorneys on the side, and eventually gave up his entrepreneurial career to focus on coaching full time.

In fact, Bousel describes a perfect storm of health issues, his newfound love for career coaching, and the growing number of disgruntled attorneys who continually sought him out as providing his own version of a website crash. "I was diagnosed with brain cancer on July 28, 1998," Bousel shared with me. "So I wanted to scale back my entrepreneurial ventures a bit. Today I am a proud brain cancer survivor. I think it's important for people to know that part of my story." Indeed, having overcome the odds, doing more than just "survive" brain cancer, the success of Art Bousel's new mission—manifested in the intensive three-day career counseling immersion provided at his Portland, Oregon, Lawyer Career Spa—shows just what happens when a tenacious, driven attorney transitions to an alternative career after a "website crash."

Of course, websites don't crash on their own. I love the "crashing website" metaphor precisely because of the involvement it requires on the part of the transitioning attorney.

You have to start and create and maintain your own "website."

You must seek out, research, and develop your own opportunities.

And be ready when they arrive.

## Notes

1. http://brickartist.com.

2. Liz Brown, J.D., *Life After Law* (Bibliomotion, 2013), at xxi.

3. *Id.* at xxii.

4. *Id.* at xxviii.

5. http://susanpackard.com/shrieks-of-ego.

6. *Id.*

7. http://www.rusticcuff.com.

8. Liz Brown, J.D., *Life After Law* (Bibliomotion, 2013), at 15.

9. *Id.* at xxviii-xxix.

10. *Id.* at xxix.

11. *Id.* at xxx.

12. *It Was Cold But It Shouldn't Have Been That Cold Inside,* Crain's Chicago Business (January 24, 1994), http://www.chicagobusiness.com/article/19940122/ISSUE01/100012952/it-was-cold-but-it-shouldnt-have-been-that-cold-inside.

# Chapter 7

# Retirement Plan
## Leaving the Workforce

*It was Leo Tolstoy who first told the world that the real secret of happiness is knowing how to love and how to work. . . . When the time of life comes to leave it [work], we must find other outlets for creativity, other sorts of work, because creativity is nourished by itself.*
—Sherwin Nuland, M.D. (1930-2014).[1]

In 2011, the first of the baby boom generation reached "retirement age." For the next 18 years, boomers will be turning 65 at a rate of about 8,000 a day.[2] Statistics show that 400,000 lawyers may retire over the next decade.[3]

Retiring lawyers face a set of issues that are arguably different from those faced by other transitioning lawyers, for whom the eventual return to practice of law may well remain a viable and real possibility. In an article written shortly after his 80th birthday, Sherwin B. Nuland, M.D., winner of the National Book Award and finalist for the Pulitzer Prize, wrote:

> To know how to work is to channel creativity into paths valuable to others and valuable to oneself. We identify with the career or occupation we have chosen, and in many ways are defined by it, seen through the eyes of the world by it. Once we have identified it when young, it in turn identifies us. Work creates an image of ourselves with which to be seen and in which to contemplate what we are. We must know how to find it, how to do it very well, and how to know

the satisfaction of presenting it to the world as a token of commitment to an ideal of quality. When the time of life comes to leave it, we must find other outlets for creativity, other sorts of work, because creativity is nourished by itself.

Our work changes as our lives and times change—especially after 65 and what we call retirement from the occupation that came before. What matters about work is neither its nature nor its formal name but the creativity and joy we put into it . . . .

Unlike life itself, the rewards of love and work are not finite. Their example becomes a gift to those who follow us; in this way they never die. And at age 25, or 65, or 85, whatever the nature of the work and of the love—it is all the same.[4]

Dr. Nuland's words ring true for retiring lawyers, who recommend that their fellow retirees heed the following advice:

1. Your retirement "plans" better include more than 80 percent of your preretirement income
2. Consider creative income-producing options for reasons other than the income
3. Be careful about agreeing to pet-sit!

## Your Retirement "Plans" Better Include More Than 80 Percent of Your Preretirement Income

The Honorable Gary Golkiewicz, former Chief Special Master of the Court of Federal Claims, knows only too well the importance of creating "work" after retirement from the "workforce." "I love working with my hands. I want to do more of that and hopefully get involved with the local Habitat for Humanity," Golkiewicz told me when we spoke in the fall of 2014. At the time, he was a prime example of just how "busy" retirement can be, working as a mediator and nearly full-time caregiver to his three-year-old grandson and his daughter's pet dog.

Golkiewicz, who from 1988 to 2010 oversaw the National Vaccine Injury Compensation Program ("Vaccine Program"),[5] retired in 2012 after 32 years of government service. In his position as Chief Special Master, Golkiewicz was instrumental in the development of the Vaccine Court and the evolution of the program over its first 20-plus years in existence; he was often turned to for informal consultation on many other proposed and developing alternative resolution programs, including those addressing radiation, asbestos, and even the September 11 claims. He was known for conducting thorough trials, fostering amicable resolutions, displaying compassionate sensitivity to the families of petitioners, and positing fair and pragmatic decisions. (I should know. I was his law clerk from 1995 to 1997.)

Indeed, in 2012, Chief Judge Rader of the Court of Appeals for the Federal Circuit noted that Golkiewicz had painstakingly "worked with Congress and many private and governmental entities to enact improvements to the program and organize an office which would successfully carry out the vision of this innovative American experiment . . . . Gary and his office exceeded expectations at every turn."

In his final four-year appointment (2008-2012), all of Golkiewicz's decisions were affirmed on appeal, in the Court of Federal Claims and the Federal Circuit, a rare feat in those years. In 2012, he was lauded by the American Academy of Pediatrics as a recipient of the Academy's 2011 Excellence in Public Service Award (EPSA), which represents the highest honor awarded by the Academy to a public servant for distinguished service to the nation's children, adolescents, and young adults. Just the year before Golkiewicz received the award, it was awarded to First Lady Michelle Obama.

For Golkiewicz, shepherding the unique Vaccine Program was a labor of love, but as his pension vesting date approached, he started researching retirement options and planning for the future. With 30 years of government service, he was eligible for retirement in 2010, two years before he ultimately left the court, and he attended a retirement conference to start planning for the future. The key advice he recalls from that conference? "Move out of Maryland," Golkiewicz laughed as he recalled that bit of practical tax advice when we spoke in 2014. In fact, he did not heed the advice when he ultimately retired in 2012, as he had two children and a grandchild in the area. Golkiewicz says: "Quality of life trumps taxes."

Nevertheless, Golkiewicz pointed out the inherent wisdom in the advice that he personally felt compelled to ignore: to consider geography and tax issues (specifically regarding 401(k)s and pensions) in making retirement plans. Experts also advise "almost retirees" to invest in a long-term health care policy while they are still working.

"If you want long-term care insurance to pay some of the cost, you'll need to health qualify, and that starts to get tricky after age 65," says Jesse Slome, executive director of the American Association for Long-Term Care Insurance. "The sweet spot is mid-50s to mid-60s [for buying these poli-cies]," according to Slome.[6]

Additionally, although the conventional advice about needing about 80 percent of preretirement income is still adhered to, experts warn not to become so obsessed with the financial plans that you forget to make other "plans" for retirement. Golkiewicz agrees. Armed with advice he refused to ignore from his own father, Golkiewicz set out to make his retirement one of "activity." "Stay active. That's the key." Golkiewicz was emphatic on that point.

Golkiewicz relayed how his father, a high-level benefits executive for the then Corning Glass Works (now Corning, Inc.) for many years, had watched with regret as too many Corning employees passed away far too soon after retirement. The senior Golkiewicz had always claimed that keeping active was a differentiator. Indeed, in 2014, Golkiewicz's father continued enjoy-ing retirement at 89, filling his days with grandchildren, bowling, golf, and other hobbies.

Following his father's lead and advice, Golkiewicz has been determined to not be still too long in his own retirement. Within four months of leav-ing the court, he began mediating—what else?—troublesome vaccine cases, noting with pride that now his mediated cases are largely brought by repeat counsel. He continues with his favorite hobbies: woodworking, babysitting, and pet-sitting (full-time!) for his two children who live locally. He says that as long as he has mediations on the calendar (no more than 10 to 12 per calendar year), he feels like he has just the right balance of "work" in his new life of "no longer working" for a living.

In sum, when making your retirement plans, by all means prepare your finances, but do not let your retirement plans stop there.

## Consider Creative Income-Producing Options
## for Reasons Other Than the Income

For now, especially after having retired at such a young age (57), Golkiewicz says he will continue to seek out income-producing opportunities. Noting that he lined up all his finances to be comfortable and secure before retirement, he enjoys drawing an additional monthly income that allows for bonuses like home redecorating projects and traveling. But Golkiewicz readily concedes that the secondary mediation career provides more than just an income supplement. He enjoys the social aspect, regularly seeing and interacting with counsel from both sides that he knew from his days on the Vaccine Court. He has also learned how much he enjoys the intellectual challenge of fostering resolutions—a practice he was always in favor of while on the court itself—as well as the travel provided by the up to 10 mediations he currently conducts per year.

In addition to mediation, Roy Ginsburg, a lawyer coach and frequent CLE presenter/speaker, points to a number of other potential income opportunities for retired lawyers that help them not only supplement their postretirement income, but also stay connected to a world they may be ambivalent about leaving—if only at first:

- Expert witness work
- Politics (running for office or working on a campaign)
- Teaching as an adjunct faculty member at a law school or college
- Teaching continuing legal education programs
- Writing articles for print or electronic media, or blogging.[7]

How much of an income supplement will you need? Some recent evidence suggests that needing 80 percent of your current salary in retirement "might be wildly exaggerated." According to David Blanchett, Morningstar's head of retirement research, "When we modeled actual spending patterns over a couple's life expectancy ... the data shows that many retirees may need approximately 20 percent less in savings."[8]

Above all, as the experts—including retired attorneys—agree when planning retirement, remember to invest as much in your intangible measures of success as you do in your financial considerations.

## Be Careful About Agreeing to Pet-Sit!

For Former Chief Special Master Gary Golkiewicz, one of his greatest joys in retirement has been the time he spends as full-time caregiver (along with his wife, a retired schoolteacher) for their three-year-old grandson. "I set up the ground rules before I agreed to watch my grandson full-time. There will be no learning or enrichment when he's with me. If my daughter wants that kind of babysitter, she'll have to pay one. This is all fun for me. And it's the most fun I've ever had."

But the dog-sitting is another issue altogether. Although Golkiewicz feels rewarded by helping his young lawyer daughter and husband as they climb their career ladders, it comes with a price. He notes that he and his wife are often tied to the house because of the dog: their activities and travel, and even outings with his grandson, can be curtailed. I've heard from other retirees, including retired lawyers, that signing on immediately as caregiver to the family pets (or even human children) might be tempting, but might also be best left to the paid professionals. As Golkiewicz warns: "The experience can be priceless, but priceless implies a cost!"

"I love being the babysitter once in a while, but I don't ever want it to feel like work," a retired lawyer grandma told me. This is why, she explains, that she loves to be her daughter's backup—but not full-time—caregiver, and why she advises friends entering retirement to look at babysitting in the same way. In fact, many experts agree that the expectations of free babysitting after retirement can be a strain on family relationships, which should be headed off early with open communication about expectations and limitations.[9]

## Notes

1. Sherwin Nuland, M.D., *Love's Labor Found*, AARP The Magazine (January 14, 2011), http://www.aarp.org/personal-growth/transitions/info-01-2011/boomers65_sherwin_nuland.html.

2. *Id.*

3. Roy S. Ginsburg, *When I'm 64: Lawyers Want to Stay "Needed" in Their Retirement Years,* http://www.royginsburg.com/when-im-64-lawyers-want-to-stay-qneededq-in-their-retirement-years.

4. Sherwin Nuland, M.D., *Love's Labor Found*, AARP The Magazine (January 14, 2011), http://www.aarp.org/personal-growth/transitions/info-01-2011/boomers65_sherwin_nuland.html.

5. The National Vaccine Program was established by the 1987 legislation entitled National Childhood Vaccine Injury Act of 1986 ("Vaccine Act"). See Pub. L. No. 99-660, 100 Stat. 3755 (1986) (codified as amended at 42 U.S.C. §§ 300aa-1 to -34). The Vaccine Program is a no-fault compensation program whereby petitions for monetary compensation may be brought by or on behalf of persons allegedly suffering injury or death as a result of the administration of certain compulsory childhood vaccines.

6. Anthony Volastro, *Retirement Myths You Need to Ignore*, CNBC.com (December 17, 2013), http://www.cnbc.com/id/101268639#.

7. Roy S. Ginsburg, *When I'm 64: Lawyers Want to Stay "Needed" in Their Retirement Years*, http://www.royginsburg.com/when-im-64-lawyers-want-to-stay-qneededq-in-their-retirement-years.

8. Anthony Volastro, *Retirement Myths You Need to Ignore*, CNBC.com (December 17, 2013), http://www.cnbc.com/id/101268639#.

9. Barbara Graham, *I'm the Grandmother, Not the Babysitter! We All Want to Help Out with the Kids, But No One Wants to Be Taken for Granted*, Grandparents.com (July 23, 2013), http://www.grandparents.com/family-and-relationships/caring%20for%20children/grandmother-not-babysitter-barbara-graham.

# Chapter 8

# Dealing with Fallout
## How to Handle Doubts and Questions
## of Colleagues, Family, and Yourself

*A seasoned prosecutor (and later trial judge) shared this story about wrapping up a death penalty case. Just before he started his well-prepared closing argument, he ripped up his notes in front of the jury, threw them on the floor, and gave what he believed to be the closing of a lifetime. While the average death penalty sentence takes 7 to 10 hours, this one came back in 30 minutes, in favor of the death penalty. This prosecutor was understandably impressed with himself.*

*"Two days later I saw the foreman in town and said, 'I just have to know, what convinced you to come back with the death penalty—and come back so quickly? Was it the way I ripped up the notes? The way I threw them on the ground? The way I got right in the defendant's face during closing?'*

*"The foreman started laughing. 'Are you kidding? Didn't you see him? The defendant was blowing kisses at the pretty female juror. We figured if he could be doing that while you were arguing for the death penalty—he probably deserved it.'*

*"The moral of this story? We are not always what we think we are."*
—Judge Todd Singer, currently a history teacher in rural North Carolina.

At the time of printing, I have been away from the practice of law for more than five years now, and in that time I have seen some real dreams come true.

I work from home. I have time to volunteer at my kids' school, serve on several influential boards, and invent new recipes for my vegan cooking club, even though I am not vegan.

I have helped grow and launch a wonderful and inspirational start-up company with a multimillion-dollar budget. My first novel, *Lemongrass Hope*, debuted as an Amazon best-seller in the fall of 2014. I have taught art history to elementary school children, and given motivational and career counseling talks to audiences ranging from elementary school children to the senior citizen students at a local university.

Nevertheless, almost monthly, someone—a family member, a friend, often my mother—will ask me: "Yes, but don't you think one day you'll go back to practicing law?"

I used to wonder, of course, when this question was asked, whether there was some gap—some wrinkle in my happiness and professional satisfaction—that others could see that I could not. I have come to realize, of course, that others cannot see what isn't there. But that won't stop people from looking for it.

I have come to accept that what people are looking at or for has nothing to do with me. It actually has to do with them.

In just the same way, it is true that the way I view the world around me actually has more to do with me than it does with the objective world around me.

Wait, this is becoming a little esoteric.

Let's talk about soap.

Do you remember the famous Dove Ad video campaign? The one that showed the women describing themselves to a forensic sketch artist, sight unseen? In that campaign, which went viral online, a forensic artist hired by Dove blindly draws women exactly as they describe themselves, and then draws the same women as described by someone whom they just met that day. Inevitably, the sketches drawn from the descriptions of strangers are softer, more flattering, and more *accurate*.

It's a powerful message.

*You are beautiful. Others see it. Why don't you?*

But, ever since first seeing this campaign online, I have always been pre-occupied by another unexplored, unknown facet to this study: namely, the strangers. How would *they* describe themselves to the sketch artist?

My guess? Probably flatteringly and accurately as well. Because I believe that we tend to see the world around us through our own filters. And the strangers portrayed in the Dove ad campaign seem open, confident, and happy, so naturally when they describe the women to the sketch artist, they describe through these open, confident, happy filters. Thus, I like to think that the strangers' self-descriptions for the sketches would also be good ones.

This whole analysis reminds me of a quote I read a few years back: "We do not see things as they are, we see them as we are." (I am fascinated by this quote largely because, depending upon the source, it is alternately attributed to Cuban-French erotica novelist Anaïs Nin or to the Talmud.)

*As we are.*

We see the world as we are.

And others see us as they are.

Which makes it impossible for us to measure our successes and failures against others' views of us.

So why even try?

Internationally famous artist Nathan Sawaya says that when he decided to leave the practice of law to be a professional Lego brick artist, the most shocked people of all were not his friends and family, but rather his colleagues. "The same people who used to commiserate with me about how much we wanted to leave the law were the most shocked when I actually left." As Sawaya points out, "Lawyers are, by nature, typically risk-averse." Many lawyers can talk incessantly about leaving, but when one actually goes through with it, it can send shock waves through the rest of the community.

Debra Vey Voda-Hamilton, founder of Hamilton Mediation Firm, jokes that some family members still don't understand why she is limiting her new practice to mediation only, as litigation is certainly more lucrative.

While I would be hard-pressed to point to any certainties in the transition from or back into the practice of law, I feel confident after hundreds of hours of research and interviews on the topic, that the following truism remains: if and when you leave the practice of law, you will need to prepare for fallout—from colleagues, from friends, from families. And from yourself.

Here are some tips for dealing with that fallout, beginning with another sure truism.

1. We are not always who we think we are—revise your imprints
2. Find your own gold stars
3. Write a book

## We Are Not Always Who We Think We Are—Revise Your Imprints

We begin with a premise that is certain to be disputed. Maybe—as Judge Singer's anecdote about his death penalty closing argument illustrates—we are not always as amazing and unbelievable as we believe we are as lawyers.

But maybe—just maybe—we can be more than we ever were.

Singer's résumé has also included positions as a former assistant and appellate public defender, former assistant district attorney, and adjunct professor of law at the University of Tulsa College of Law. This accomplished lawyer told me about the day—at a Father's Day picnic, in fact—that his son's teacher shared with him a project from school. His son had filled in questions posed by his teacher:

My dad's favorite color is: ____ black.

My dad's favorite food is: ___ I don't know. He eats alone.

Soon after that picnic, Singer left the bench and began focusing on full-time lobbying/consulting work, which freed up more time for family and other pursuits. Still, Singer says he wouldn't find his true professional calling until more than a decade later. According to Singer, "[I]n a way, it took me until age 52 to really know what I wanted to do when I grew up."

Singer says he just always knew there was more to him than that loving-black-and-eating-alone dad described by his son. In 2011, he finally moved to North Carolina to teach in an underserved community, fulfilling a long-held dream of his.

"These kids are brilliant in how they endure life. How they push through seemingly insurmountable obstacles. I'm so enriched by them.

"Kids are honest. They are not trying to delay a hearing because they are not prepared.

On some level, I am hoping to elevate a sense of wonder in them."

Casey Berman, founder of the "Leave Law Behind" blog, also provides some helpful insight on this topic. Citing the philosophy of John Kehoe, a best-selling author and authority on positive thinking, Berman believes that our attitude and perception and the thoughts we think empower, or sabotage, our real-life, tangible actions and goals. Berman points out that if true, Kehoe's belief that repeated thoughts "imprint" on our subconscious can translate into some very real—and, I trust, familiar—thoughts for attorneys. Just a few cited by Berman include:

- Working hard means respect
- You are happy when the client is happy
- The skills you have as a lawyer can only be used as a lawyer
- Stress is a badge of honor[1]

Berman suggests revising those imprints for attorneys, and I cite here just a few of his suggestions:

- When I work at a role where I am always using my skills and strengths, I'll be a huge success
- People need me and value me
- I expect to spend time with my family
- Good things happen to me
- Being creative can be better and more lucrative than working hard
- Take time to think
- Create
- Get a job that fits us well[2]

As Berman says poignantly: "No one has ever done well—financially, emotionally, psychologically—at a job they don't like. They make a living, but they don't make a life."

The main reason, of course, that the questions and fallout from those within and outside the law can be so scathing is that as lawyers, we believe that our identity is truly tied to the mere fact that we are lawyers. Lawyers measure their worth in billable hours, trial wins, motions granted. And when you give those measures up—however temporarily—you may find yourself struggling to answer the question *who am I now?*

It's OK. Struggle with it.

Answer it.

For former judge Singer, prior wins and successes pale in comparison to what he is accomplishing now. Last semester, his history class, for example, took on the living assignment of attempting to trace a letter from a Holocaust victim to any living relatives/descendants. Singer, along with his wife, began collecting Holocaust artifacts in 2000, compiling the items into an exhibit that they donated to the Holocaust Museum. Recently, he came across a letter from a Betty Erb in Berlin to a John Erb in Philadelphia, dated 1939, and brought the letter to his class for the assignment. He notes that even students who usually are not very engaged in class have committed deeply to the project.[3]

As Singer says, "We are not always who we think we are." As Singer has proven, we might be much more.

## Find Your Own Gold Stars

I have learned over time that there are two kinds of people in this world:

People who don't need gold stars.

And me.

It's true. When I work hard, succeed in some small way, or reach the end of a project, I like someone to reach in their desk, pull out a sheet of shiny gold star stickers and slap one across my work.

I don't need monetary or other rewards, phony praise, *quid pro quo*, public acknowledgment. Nothing like that.

Just a gold star.

Something that says: Hey, that mattered. It really did.

It's not that I don't genuinely enjoy working hard, or doing helpful things. I do. But without the gold star, I've always found it hard to know if what

I did or am doing matters. And I'm not alone in this. It's a common trait among lawyers, I have discovered.

Many transitioning lawyers report feeling the lack of validation or rewards when they leave the active practice of law—a loss that has nothing to do with salary or income.

In a 2013 *New York Times Magazine* article profiling high-profile women who had left their professional lives more than a decade earlier, Judith Warner, the *New York Times* best-selling author of *Perfect Madness*, reported:

> But money was not the primary focus of the women I spoke with—whether they needed more of it or not. Rather, what haunted many of them, as they reckoned with the past 10 years of their lives, was a more unquantifiable sense of personal change. They had been supremely self-confident when they took the "plunge into full-time motherhood," as a former high-level corporate lawyer put it to me. (Like a few of the other women I talked to, she didn't want to be identified—she was newly re-employed and didn't want attention brought to her years out of the workforce.)[4]

Warner says: "The longer they're home, the more they continue the trajectory toward something different . . . . They have greater appreciation of some of the values of home and connectivity, which were somewhat alien to them in their high-flying professions."[5]

In 2012, I organized an enormous relief effort for my former town of Rockaway, New York, after the devastating aftermath of Hurricane Sandy. The relief effort began really as an accident. An email I sent to a few friends to try to gather supplies for the town, which had been ravaged by floods and fires in the past few days, went viral in 24 hours, and eventually I had to turn away donations when my three-car garage was filled to the brim twice over with clothing, blankets, and supplies. A friend and I hand-delivered the supplies in a heartbreaking trip that nearly crushed my spirit: so great was the devastation, so small a dent did the supplies seem to make that day. Even amid the darkness and destruction, I met so many beautiful people throughout the day, who said continual, heartfelt thank-yous.

But all I could keep saying was, "No. It's nothing. Really."

To be honest, I was heartbroken for a long time, thinking that none of it—none of what I had personally organized, retrieved, gathered, delivered, or done had really mattered.

No gold stars.

Fast-forward nearly a year later, to 2013. On a trip to Costa Rica, I found myself very seasick on a boat trip—something that I almost never am. A crewmember brought me some relief—warm soda and crackers. "Senorita, take some crackers. You'll feel better soon."

I was green and queasy lying in the middle of a catamaran off the west coast of Costa Rica, and a crew member named Luis had suddenly become my best friend. My kids were standing nearby watching for wildlife off the side of the boat. I took the crackers and sipped a Coke while Luis watched me with an attentive smile. I was so very grateful for these small, simple gestures on the part of a stranger.

"Thank you, Luis. *Gracias.*"

Before he could respond, one of my kids asked, "How do you say 'you're welcome' in Spanish? It's '*de nada,*' right?"

Luis's smile evaporated as he scowled at them. "No, no. That's not what we say here. '*De nada*' means 'it's nothing.'" He practically spit out the words "*de nada*" and "nothing."

"Here in Costa Rica, we say '*con mucho gusto.*' It means 'with much pleasure, much happiness.' So much better—no?"

Soon after meeting Luis, when my husband and I took our kids back to Rockaway, New York, to deliver school supplies and spend some money and time in the newly opened mom-and-pop stores across the island, we were able to witness the amazing rebuilding effort in a town known for its resilience and character. I thought about Luis, his crackers and Coke and kind smile, and how all I could keep saying on that 2012 day on which we had brought in relief supplies was: "It's nothing."

As my family left Rockaway that 2013 summer day, I noticed the signs decorating the telephone poles on every corner of the town, still up eight months after the hurricane.

Stars.

Blue stars—not gold, but still.

I have learned from Luis and Rockaway, and from my years away from the practice of law, that it is not always easy to find the gold stars when you leave. They are not always as transparent as successful summary judgment motions and winning verdicts. They are no longer measured in settlement leverage or favorable negotiations.

But there will be stars. You just have to look for them. And, by the way, they just might be blue.

*Con mucho gusto.*

## Write a Book

Or start a nonprofit. Or volunteer for the local homeless shelter. Or run a marathon. Or organize a community group to clean the local playground. Or make jewelry. Or join a vegan cooking club.

In other words: Give them something else to talk about.

They may well always continue to ask you: *Don't you think you'll go back to practicing law?*

You may never really know the answer to that question. But you can give them something else to talk about in the meantime. And yourself, for that matter.

Brian Kamoie, appointed by President Barack Obama in 2013 as the assistant administrator for Grant Programs of the Federal Emergency Management Agency, talks about leaving the prestigious law firm Proskauer Rose to teach. Ultimately, he both taught and worked at the White House for four years before his FEMA appointment. "I went from being a lawyer to being the client—which was much more fun." Kamoie offers this as his explanation of why he never really suffered from that all-too-familiar identity crisis many other transitioning attorneys describe.

Erin Giglia, co-founder of Montage Legal Group, knows well the identity issues that attorneys face when they think about transitioning from the law. Giglia, who had come from a background of struggle and poverty, had chosen a legal career precisely for the long-term stability it could potentially provide. She was extremely reluctant to give up that stability. "I felt I was letting myself down. I felt like one of the women I now talk to every day, who feels that they will lose their identity. That they are somehow failing themselves, and all women who came before them."

How did she deal with that identity issue? Well, when Giglia finally decided to transition from the full-time practice of law (after some time of having one toe out the door, she concedes) to join her friend, Laurie, in the freelance legal world, she asked, "How can we make this bigger? How can we think beyond ourselves?" For Giglia, staying connected to the legal profession helps mitigate the identity issue that she believes becomes more pronounced in those who leave the field altogether. When I asked Giglia the question I ask all my transitioning attorney interviewees—"If someone comes up to you at a cocktail party and asks if you are a lawyer, what do you say?"—Erin gave me an unflinching and enthusiastic "I say yes!"

A *Forbes* article called Erin and her friend Laurie "stay-at-home moms,"[6] and in a way they are. Just as I am. I stay home with my kids instead of leaving them in full-time child care to go to an office to work each day, and that's what distinguishes Erin and Laurie's current lives from their prior ones as well. But not the workload. They still work long hours, and Giglia has even been known to "practice" law on occasion. "When a client has an emergency, or specifically requests me," she says. "Then I will jump in and do the project work myself."

And despite the *Forbes* characterization of Erin and Laurie as "stay-at-home moms," Giglia says that no one ever asks her whether she will go back to practicing law.

"What's your secret?" I have to ask her, "because *everyone* seems to ask me that. Still."

She says, "When you have a business, when you are a successful entrepreneur . . . no one asks you" if you intend to go back to the life you had before.

*When you give them something else to talk about, that is what they will talk about.*

Simple, really. Don't you think?

## Notes

1. Casey Berman, *The Horns Blare and the Drums Beat and Your Power Is Now Limitless,* LeaveLawBehind.com (September 13, 2014).

2. *Id.*

3. Molly McGowan, *East Students Trace History of Holocaust Letter*, BlueRidgeNow.com (April 27, 2014), http://www.blueridgenow.com/article/20140427/ARTICLES/140429903/0/search.

4. Judith Warner, *The Opt-Out Generation Wants Back In*, N.Y. Times Magazine (August 7, 2013), http://www.nytimes.com/2013/08/11/magazine/the-opt-out-generation-wants-back-in.html?pagewanted=all&_r=0.

5. *Id.*

6. Mamie Joeveer, *How Two Stay-at-Home-Moms Are Changing the Legal Industry*, Forbes.com (August 27, 2014).

# Chapter 9

# Ethical and Practical Considerations

*Do you have a partner or an investor?*

*No. I never wanted an investor . . . . But I have several wonderful mentors. And I consult often with an expert on ethics. I think that's really important.*

—Genavieve Shingle, founder, Damsel in Defense

It would be irresponsible to discuss transitions from the practice of law without addressing the ethical and practical issues relevant to such transitions. Of course, it would be similarly irresponsible to suggest that this chapter provides comprehensive ethical advice, and in fact many ethics experts were reluctant to have their advice be quoted in piecemeal form herein. Consequently, this chapter is intended to raise the issues, to help you recognize and consider them, and to encourage you to seek ethics advice where appropriate. Which I know you will, because, let's face it, we lawyers are generally a risk-averse bunch, no matter how much we try to pretend otherwise.

1. The clients, and files, and money—Oh my!
2. Be careful at cocktail parties
3. Know the *pro bono* rules in your state
4. Keep your license active

## The Clients, and Files, and Money—Oh My!

Experts (and ABA Formal Opinion 99-4143) agree that when you are leaving your firm—however temporarily—you should make sure to work with your firm in preparing communication with your direct clients about your impending absence, and their right to choose their own attorney. If you are leaving to practice at a new firm, your clients have the right to follow you if they choose. If you are leaving so as not to practice any longer, they have the right to hire a new firm altogether.[1]

Thus, it is advisable to communicate with existing clients through joint written notice from lawyer and firm, and client communications should clearly advise them of their right to decide who will continue on in their representation. Communications should not be disparaging, and should not urge the client to sever the relationship with the existing firm, but it is permissible to advise the client of the continued availability of representation with the existing lawyer, and provide other information about the transitioning lawyer's new firm (such as fees) that will help the clients make an informed decision about their continued representation.[2]

In their April 2000 article, "Fifty Ways to Leave Your Law Firm," Roger Geller and Susan Strauss Weisberg write: "[T]he firm must not prevent the departing lawyer from honoring these obligations or attempt to thwart any ongoing relationships between that lawyer and departing clients. We frequently hear from departing lawyers, often younger associates, that their employers have forbidden them to announce their departure, notify their clients or opposing counsel, or take other appropriate measures to protect the clients. Firm personnel have been instructed not to disclose the whereabouts of former lawyers to departing clients or other callers. Remaining lawyers have impermissibly withheld the files of departing clients as leverage in disputes with departing lawyers over the division of fees or other lawyer-to-lawyer issues."[3]

Make sure you file all appropriate withdrawals (even when you have co-counsel) in order to comply with ethical obligations to your client, and protect yourself from ongoing liability in a case on which you are no longer working. In addition to the formally required communications, make sure to communicate honestly and fairly about your future plans, especially with the clients you have had the most dealings with. Beyond the ethical considerations, they are contacts whom you will want to look up later on. They are not bridges to burn.

Laurel Bellows, past president of the American Bar Association from 2012 to 2013, tells how she broke the news to her clients as she began the important transition of leaving her practice for a year to carry out her duties as ABA president. "I prepared clients with news of this tremendous honor during my year as president-elect, being certain to introduce them to colleagues whenever possible. I spoke with clients about the national and international platform that the American Bar Association provides and the opportunity for me to make a difference on issues that were important to me such as: national cybersecurity, gender equity and the fight against modern day slavery in the US . . . . Clients were supportive and favorably impressed that their lawyer was elected president of the American Bar Association. They spread the word to their friends and were proud to refer the firm business at every opportunity."

Bellows also reports that while away from her practice carrying out her duties as ABA president, she "checked in directly on pending matters, called clients as often as possible and tried to be involved in strategy discussions, delegating implementation to colleagues with my oversight." As for colleague preparation prior to her transition, Bellows gave substantial time to that endeavor as well. "After election, we began additional practical training at no additional charge to clients. I engaged a colleague to become involved in every new matter brought into the firm. . . . Colleagues were favorable, supportive and enjoyed the added level of responsibility and direct client contact."

Wondering which files and money you should take prior to a transition? Ethics opinions dictate that the files belong to the client and the money belongs to whoever earned it. So, what should you take? Take only information about your previously represented clients to do a conflicts check, and files for clients who are following you after informed consent. Same goes for the fees. A New York Court of Appeals decision held (unanimously) that under state law, a law firm "does not own a client or an engagement and is only entitled to be paid for services actually rendered."[4]

When it comes to clients, their files, and the money, by all means, consult with ethical rules. But consider also that there are practical considerations beyond the ethical obligations that will make your transition away easier. Should you decide to return, these measures will make your transition back to the practice easier as well.

## Be Careful at Cocktail Parties

One of the most common situations every attorney finds himself or herself in is the cocktail party conversation where someone is asking for legal advice. When you have an office or an affiliate law firm, you can easily put the party guest off by asking them to call you at the office Monday morning. But a transitioning attorney may not have an office, and thus may not have that luxury any longer. Complicating the situation further—depending on how you plan to spend your time away from the law—you will have more time now for cocktail parties, and for online networking and blog forums, where this type of casual "trolling" for legal advice is even more prevalent.

The answer is simple to say—harder to do.

*Don't give casual legal advice.*

There is a big difference between "You should seek out a trusts & estates attorney, I have some friends who practice in that area," and "Yep, you should definitely sue your sister."

Of course, casual legal advice may involve you in the bigger issue, where you don't just say, you also do. In which case, the next section might become relevant.

## Know the *Pro Bono* Rules in Your State

It goes without saying that during your transition time, you should not take on active legal work without maintaining some type of malpractice insurance and an active license.

But what about the active paid practice of law's kissing cousin, *pro bono* work? Surely you should be able to review your brother-in-law's real estate documents, and your neighbor's father's will, without procuring malpractice insurance?

In a word, it's a *risk*.

There are states that make it easier than others for retired and inactive attorneys to take on *pro bono* work, including through limited insurance policies, affiliation with an organization such as Legal Aid, or similar group.

Some jurisdictions even allow retired or inactive lawyers to provide *pro bono* services. Illinois, for example, modified its rules in 2008 to give retired, inactive, and corporate attorneys limited admission status to provide on a *pro bono* basis critical legal assistance to vulnerable and disadvantaged people who would otherwise be shut out of the justice system. In Illinois, these attorneys must provide *pro bono* services under the auspices of a sponsoring entity, which is defined as "a not-for-profit legal services organization, governmental entity, law school clinical program or a bar association providing *pro bono* services."[5]

In New York in 2010, the court system enlisted retired lawyers to offer free legal advice and representation to poor New Yorkers in foreclosure, debt collection, housing, family and other civil cases. They are not subject to the state's attorney registration fee or mandatory CLE requirements, and receive free training and malpractice insurance coverage from the agencies or under the state Public Officers Law.[6]

In sum, if you are retiring or going inactive, and still would like to do *pro bono* work, check your particular state's rules first. Many retiring attorneys purchase what is called a "tail" malpractice policy or an "extended reporting period (ERP)," which covers claims made during the time period of the tail (usually three to seven years).

There are restrictions and limitations for certain tail policies, however (*e.g.,* they may only cover work of actively licensed attorneys), so you will need to consult with your broker or insurer on the scope of the policy specifically in connection with your anticipated *pro bono* activities.[7]

## Keep Your License Active

Because many transitioning and departing attorneys feel compelled to let their licenses and/or CLE attendance lag immediately following their departure, it is important to consider, at the beginning of a break, whether you will want to do so. There are a number of reasons not to—not the least of which is wanting the ability to resume the practice of law fairly quickly if the opportunity arises.

Amy Gewirtz, director of New Directions for Attorneys—a program for attorney re-entry—says that she advises all New Directions participants to reactivate their licenses upon joining the program, for just that reason. A candidate who is ready to jump right back in is more attractive to potential recruiters. Before automatically checking the "inactive" box on your state attorney license registration forms, call your state's bar to find out what the requirements are for inactive status. Can you be inactive for some period of time (*e.g.*, three years?) before a formal motion for active status must be made? While inactive, can you defer your annual CLE requirements for some period of time without penalty?

Once you go to all of this work to establish your inactive status, don't pretend that you are active. Don't give legal advice, or work for a company where your job description is "attorney" even if it isn't explicitly stated so. When I started working for a start-up company after I left my position at Skadden Arps, it was often joked that it was good to have a resident attorney around. And while I embraced the fact that as a trained attorney, I could evaluate issues with a critical mind, write persuasive pitches, and successfully negotiate the best possible pricing with vendors, I also was careful at all times not to give legal advice, and to refer any questions even bordering on legal advice questions to the in-house law department of our parent company.

Be careful about holding yourself out as an active attorney. Remember, though, while you transition from the active practice of law, that there are certain ethical and practical reasons you might want to hold onto the trappings of an active attorney, including insurance, CLE credits, and active licenses.

## Notes

1. Lynda C. Shely, *Law Firm Changes: The Ethical Obligations When Lawyers Switch Firms*, ABA 32nd National Conference on Professional Responsibility Coursebook (June 2006); ABA Formal Op. 99-4143.

2. ABA Formal Op. 99-4143; ABA Informal Ops. 1457 (April 29, 1980) and 1466 (February 12, 1981).

3. Roger Geller & Susan Strauss Weisberg, *Fifty Ways to Leave Your Law Firm,* Mass.gov (April 2000), http://www.mass.gov/obcbbo/fifty.htm.

4. *In re Thelen LLP,* 2014 NY slip op 04879 (Ct. App. decided July 1, 2014).

5. American Bar Association, Standing Committee on Lawyers' Professional Liability, *Pro Bono Work and Malpractice Coverage: A Guide for the Pro Bono Attorney* (April 2013).

6. *Id.*

7. *Id.*

# Chapter 10

# On the Road Again
## After a Break

*I always wanted to work for [Live Aid producer] Bill Graham. Even after he died, I called and called his office asking about available opportunities and was repeatedly turned down. One day I drove halfway across the country to the office, showed up unannounced, and was offered a low-level three-month position.*

*As an intern.*

*It wasn't exactly my dream job.*

*I said: "I'm kind of a lawyer."*

*And a guy there told me: "There's no other way."*

*I took the internship, worked hard, and on the last day of my low-level three-month internship stint, I was offered a position going on the road with the Rolling Stones.*

*Exactly. The Rolling Stones.*

—Marc Luber, founder of the award-winning video website, JDCareersOutThere.com

If you eventually relaunch your interrupted legal career, it is important to be as thoughtful about your re-entry as you were about your original transition. As *Back on the Career Track* co-authors Carol Cohen and Vivian Rabin say, "[U]nlike the choice to purse nonwork passions, the decision to return to work has the distinction of not being completely on your own terms. It involves an obligation to others beyond your family and you. The last thing you want to do is take on a professional commitment and not deliver. Therefore make sure you decide whether or not to return to work not by default, but after exhausting all other ways you may want to spend your time."[1] It is important not to relaunch your career too soon. In truth, your commitment to relaunching your career may well determine your success, rather than the years spent outside of the legal field.

Amy Gewirtz is director of New Directions for Attorneys at Pace Law School, a re-entry program launched in 2007 to help lawyers transition back into the workforce. Gewirtz knows the hurdles to relaunching well. And they are not what you might think.

Gewirtz says one of the biggest hurdles for lawyers who have been out of the profession for a number of years is *not* necessarily the years they have been away. In fact, while her program has helped lawyers return to their legal careers after three and four years out, Gewirtz reports that program participants more commonly have been out of the profession anywhere from 7 to 30 years. Gewirtz and other relaunching experts agree that technology advances can pose a bigger challenge than getting up to speed on the legal issues, so there are clearly other factors at work in the relative success or failure to relaunch a legal career once you decide to do so.

Should finances be a factor in relaunching? Well, certainly some might find that they have to go back to work due to changes in personal or financial situations. And since most experts agree that the longer a lawyer is away from the profession, the more of a long-term negative impact on salary occurs, these would be factors best considered at the start of a break—that is, at the time the transitioning attorney first emerges from the practice of law for a sabbatical or for an unpaid choice such as caregiving. But at the time of re-entry, it would seem futile to dwell on or try to reverse the facts about the numbers or the salary impact; better to simply address the viability of re-entering at all.

To that end, it appears that the most helpful advice at the point of re-entry is not to focus on the potential negative salary implications of your time off. It is also not that helpful to tell relaunching lawyers to follow their passions blindly. It is not universally helpful to say things like "age doesn't matter" or that you should follow only your passions. Sometimes, as Gewirtz helpfully suggests, you have to be a little practical in your goals for re-entering the profession after years away.

At least for a little while.

At least in the beginning.

All of the best advice to attorneys seeking to transition back into the practice of law can be boiled down to these six items.

1. Say your number out loud
2. Low-level interns might go out on tour with the Rolling Stones
3. Don't go back too soon
4. It's the technology (that makes you feel) stupid
5. It's all about who you know
6. Know who you are

## Say Your Number Out Loud

As *Life After Law* author Liz Brown advises, right at the beginning of formulating your re-entry plan, you need to articulate your minimum salary requirements out loud. Instead of hoping for some ratio of your previous salary before you left the law, or trying to put a number on what you think your previous experience and current résumé are "worth," start by articulating what you actually need to live on. Factor in child care and other new expenses that working will introduce into your budget, including commuting, clothing, and food expenses. Move or downsize if you can or if you have to.

And then say the number out loud.

Own it so that when a great position comes along—and it will—with a not-so-large dollar sign attached to it, you will be able to accept it without salary hang-ups.

In 2011, after working as a freelance consultant and writer for a new start-up company named Hybrid Her for several years, I was offered a position as director of Community & Content. The company had been named one of *Forbes Woman*'s Best Websites for Women in 2010 and was poised to reclaim the title for 2011, based on innovative work creating an e-commerce component of the site called the "Bazaar" that I was helping to run. Hybrid Her boasted a dynamic creative team and an enthusiastic and supportive investor. The company's mission of supporting, recruiting, and engaging women entrepreneurs was one I believed in fiercely. And the co-founder, Beth Smith, was a mentor to me and a wonderful collaborative partner. I was able to work entirely from home, participating in team meetings virtually, and I was invited into the central decision-making core team of the company—invited to make a real impact on the brand's development and future iteration.

It was a dream job.

It was also a frugal start-up company and the offered salary was a fraction of the hefty six-figure law firm salary I had left behind in 2009. And when I say "fraction" I mean *small* fraction.

"We can't offer you anything close to what you're used to, what you're worth, frankly," the business director said apologetically as she offered me about 10 percent of my prior law firm salary. Luckily, I had already done the calculations of what salary I would actually "require" for my dream job. It was a little higher than what I had been offered, but not much. I asked for "my" number, received it, and within a year or two, as the company continued to grow, so did my love for my decision. Perhaps not coincidentally, so did my salary.

In the meantime, I had done something that made the financial issue almost a moot point. I had moved.

On June 1, 2010, literally (and symbolically) on the first anniversary of leaving my corporate litigator position at Skadden Arps, my husband and I closed on a new home in rural Pennsylvania, deliberately leaving behind our more expensive life in New York, so that our "numbers" would be smaller if need be.

I once asked Gretchen Rubin, former practicing attorney and best-selling author of *The Happiness Project*, if she believed that geography played any significant part in a person's happiness equation. She answered that "all relevant research indicates no" while equivocating: "But that doesn't really seem right—no?"

When I told Rubin about my and my husband's conscious decision to relocate from a place we loved—New York—to a new place we thought we could grow to love in a different way, she smiled and responded, "Well, to some, rural Pennsylvania may seem ideal, and to others it may seem like the Ninth Circle of Hell—right?"

I had to concede that she was right. You may indeed affect your happiness equation by removing or mitigating financial impediments after transitioning from the practice of law—and before transitioning back—but you have to decide whether this means leaving the state, or just moving from a four-bedroom, two-story colonial into a comfortable studio apartment in the same town. Either way, try to reduce your "number" as low as comfortably possible.

New Directions Director Amy Gewirtz says that when doing so is indeed economically viable, "successful relaunchers will demonstrate ability and willingness to accept lower salary." Articulating your number realistically may very well free you up to opportunities you might have dismissed on the salary basis alone.

There are sacrifices to be made in committing to re-enter the legal profession, and as Hollee Temple, former litigator and co-author of *Good Enough Is the New Perfect,* points out, your sacrifices should mirror your priorities. Temple took more than a 50 percent salary cut in leaving her law firm position to pursue a career in teaching. She didn't even have a "professor" title at first, and it took five years to convert to a professor title track. But when I spoke with her in the summer of 2014, she was teaching and starting a new entrepreneurial venture, known as the Beauty Bar, and said she couldn't be happier.

It hadn't happened overnight, of course. When I first spoke with Temple, she was in her 11th year of teaching. The transition back into the profession also takes sacrifice and patience. And, perhaps most importantly, as *Life After Law* author Liz Brown says, "You need to learn how to separate your self-worth from your income." In other words, my fellow lawyers, you need to unlearn a key tenet from law firm life, especially big firm life. You are *not*—contrary to what you have always been taught to believe—worth only as much as the dollars you bring in.

Once you establish your minimum salary requirements, you can align your priorities accordingly. Articulating this number (out loud!) will help you follow tip number 2 more seamlessly and painlessly.

## Low-Level Interns Might Go Out on Tour with the Rolling Stones

It would sound lovely to say "follow your passions" when relaunching your career. It would probably sound much more soothing to advise you to not settle. To make your time off meaningful by waiting to go back until your dream job presents itself—gift-wrapped.

But that would be pointless.

I do not believe that is sound advice, and neither does relaunching expert Amy Gewirtz. I nearly hugged Gewirtz when she said to me, "[Y]ou know, sometimes you have to put a pin in your passions and be practical." That is really a summation of all of the best relaunching advice I have ever heard.

You have been out of the workforce for $x$ amount of years. Others have remained. You should not be punished for leaving. They shouldn't be punished for staying.

Instead of begrudging the revised hierarchical roles you may find yourself being offered in the relaunching world, remember that some younger people you may have to report to have now been there longer than you, and strive to see the position as one of mutual benefit. They will have fresh new ideas and technological skills to impart. They will know about the industry, but you will have fresh eyes too. You will have life experience.

As Liz Brown says, "the key is to remain flexible so you know when to pivot . . . . Know what's nonnegotiable and what brings you joy. It is not likely to be salary or job titles."

Relaunching expert Carol Cohen, co-founder of iRelaunch and co-author of *Back on the Career Track,* also agrees that relaunching professionals—and especially relaunching lawyers—need to be clever and perhaps a bit humble in their relaunching strategies. Embracing the concept of "strategic volunteerism" addressed in Chapter 1, Cohen says that she has seen great success stories from attorneys who took on low-paying or even unpaid positions that led to part-time and full-time positions back into the legal profession. She cautions that those who are determined "not to settle" need to be honest about their intentions and motivations.

A recent blog entry on Ms. JD, titled "Keep Not Settling," says:

I'm still looking for work, and I'm hopeful that I'll find something soon. But I want that something to be great, not just something I have to take simply because it beats unemployment. For the past few years, that's been my mentality.

I would truly rather have a job that makes me happy and pays me peanuts over a job that I hate but pays me well. But in this economy and with copious amounts of student loan debt we often feel forced to settle for whatever we can get, happiness be damned.

The danger with that is we attract what we seek. So if we keep going after things we don't truly love, we're going to keep getting things we don't love. I've applied for both jobs I really want and jobs that I know I'd hate, and I'm still unemployed. Focusing solely on jobs that I know I really want won't hurt my chances of employment going forward.[2]

All beautiful-sounding sentiments. But again, the author is still unemployed. After several years. Not necessarily a desired outcome.

When deciding to return to the legal field after more than a decade away from her practice, Camille Raia sought out her own internship in the health care field to make a reality of her dream of entering a sector of the law that she perceived as booming. Raia enrolled in the New Directions program in 2012 and even though there were no advertised externships in the legal/medical field she sought to join, she pursued a position on her own, applied for it, and ultimately got a position at Hackensack Medical Center. "When you're hungry enough," Raia points out, "you can achieve more." Eventually, the experience Raia gained in the health care law field enabled her to join Platinum Health Care as an independent contractor, where she was hired on in her current position as general counsel after proving herself in only three months. Raia notes that in her time away she was extremely involved in her community, and those networks helped her rejoin the workforce, although she credits New Directions and the contacts she made there as "key."

Think unpaid internships and proving yourself are beneath you? Sometimes, as iRelaunch's Carol Cohen, New Directions's Amy Gewirtz, and others have noted, we have to lower our arbitrary "bar" somewhat.

Don't believe me? Ask Marc Luber, founder of the award-winning blog JDCareersOutThere.com. Early on in his professional journey, Luber became inspired by the professional track of Bill Graham, producer of the 1985 Live Aid Concert, and wrote to Graham asking for mentorship and advice. Luber says that in return, he received a letter from Graham that "changed his life." Graham told him to go to law school or business school and to "do lots of internships."

Luber took Graham's words to heart and sought out positions at *Spin* magazine, and later was a summer associate for what was then RCA Records. He even worked for the manager of Crosby Stills & Nash, all the while hoping that his path would eventually lead to a position in Graham's company.

And then, tragically, Graham died in 1991, and Luber was devastated.

Luber decided to take Graham's advice again, and sought an internship with Graham's company, in the wake of the founder's death. He was turned down repeatedly by phone and mail, but instead of giving up, Luber decided to make the drive from Chicago to California and request a position in person.

Luber shares a fabulous anecdote: "I was having breakfast at a diner right before my driving to the Bill Graham office. I was reading the new *Rolling Stone* magazine with the Smashing Pumpkins on the cover. By coincidence, they walked in and sat at the table next to me while I was having breakfast. I took that as a sign of good luck!"

Luber drove halfway across the country to request a position with Graham's company in person, and he ended up taking the only position offered: a low-level, nonlegal internship position, which he accepted after pointing out that "I'm kind of a lawyer." On the last day of that internship, Luber was offered—and took!—a chance to tour with the Rolling Stones, which led to various full-time, and increasingly lucrative positions in the music industry over the next years. Now Luber's business, a video website called JDCareersOutThere.com, is truly the culmination of his legal training and experience in the entertainment industry—an intersection he came to through continuous self-assessment, hard work, and strategic internships.

Justice Sandra Day O'Connor relayed to Carol Cohen and Vivian Rabin, co-founders of iRelaunch, how she successfully relaunched the way she wanted: to a part-time position, in 1965 when such arrangements were nonexistent for lawyers. After having left the profession for five years to raise her two sons, O'Connor joined the Arizona Attorney General's office.

She felt lucky to have the job because she had been virtually unemployable prior to her transition to caregiving. Although she had graduated third in her class at Stanford, at that time women lawyers faced stiff hurdles to employment, and O'Connor says that few private firms would even interview her—certainly none would offer her a job. She ended up starting her own general practice with a partner before leaving to become a full-time caregiver for five years.

But when O'Connor rejoined the profession, she wanted to do so on her own terms. So she struck an interesting deal. "I loved the job. It was the most fun I had in my career." But she wanted to work part-time, not full-time, so O'Connor made a bold move. "First I tried to make myself indispensable. Then I proposed working two-thirds time. I told them I would make them a great deal, because they'd only have to pay me for half time and I'd work two-thirds time. Thus one of the original less-than-full-time legal paths was created." Today O'Connor remains "the only Supreme Court justice who relaunched her career."[3]

Many relaunching attorneys talk about the freedom they felt to ask questions, to gain confidence, to make mistakes, and—most importantly—*to learn* during the transition period during which they "interned" or took a position for which they were arguably overqualified and underpaid.

Caren Ulrich Stacy touted the benefits of such an arrangement as we talked in the fall of 2014 about her program, OnRamp Fellowship, which had just recently expanded exponentially. After working as a recruiter for several law firms and seeing how difficult it was to place high-performing, highly credentialed lateral attorneys who had "gaps" on their résumés for caregiving years, Stacy decided to start OnRamp Fellowship, a one-year fellowship program for relaunching attorneys. She admits that some have criticized the fact that fellowship participants receive compensation from top law firms of $125,000—less than the market salary for lateral attorneys at these same firms.

OnRamp Fellowship's success is premised on the idea that:

The legal profession has a leaky pipeline. Plenty of high-performing lawyers enter the legal profession. But many of these lawyers—women in particular—leave within a few years. In Am Law 200 firms, for instance, there is typically a 50/50 gender split at the entry-level, but only 16 percent of partners are women.

Once these women lawyers exit the profession, it's not easy to get back in. Since law firms usually hire and advance lawyers based on tenure, it's difficult for a returning lawyer and her potential employer to know where she fits into the traditional structure upon re-entry. And, in most law firms, it is virtually impossible for an experienced lawyer to re-engineer her practice because of the rigid billable rate structure that is typically tied to years of experience. This structure forces skilled lawyers who are not a fit for their current practice area to change jobs or exit the profession for other opportunities.

A 2010 study by the Center for Work-Life Policy found that 73 percent of women trying to return to the workforce after a voluntary timeout for childcare or other reasons have difficulty finding a job.[4]

Stacy's OnRamp Fellowship is billed as "a re-entry platform that matches experienced lawyers returning to the profession with law firms for a one-year, paid training contract. This unique experiential learning program gives returning women lawyers—many of whom have opted out of the legal field for a period of time to raise children—an opportunity to demonstrate their value in the marketplace while also increasing their experience, skills, and legal contacts."[5]

In short, it's a way back in. For less money? Sure. But it is coupled with training, mentorship, and the type of gradual transition (including reduced billable requirements) that many relaunching attorneys say is a differentiator for success.

Is OnRamp Fellowship a tremendous value to its participants (both firms and lawyers)? You bet. The program began in 2014 with four firms, Baker Botts LLP, Cooley LLP, Hogan Lovells LLP, and Sidley Austin LLP, as an "experiment." When the experiment proved successful, 11 additional firms joined the program in late 2014: Akerman LLP; Baker, Donelson, Bearman, Caldwell & Berkowitz PC; Blank Rome LLP; Crowell & Moring LLP; Fenwick & West LLP; Fish & Richardson PC; Fried, Frank, Harris, Shriver & Jacobson LLP; Jenner & Block LLP; K&L Gates LLP; Orrick, Herrington & Sutcliffe LLP; and White & Case LLP.

As for the innovative New Directions for Attorneys program at Pace Law School, the graduates I spoke to universally credited the program's three-month externship component with their later success in relaunching. Take, for example, Susan Taylorson, a New Directions graduate and an attorney now practicing real estate law. Taylorson gave high praise to not just her own unpaid externship, but the concept in general. She notes that while her externship workload was intense and substantive, given her status as an unpaid extern, she felt free to ask questions. Some pressure of being expected to know everything, especially on the technology front, was eased up a bit.

New Directions graduate (and later assistant director) Caroll Welch says you should not give away your value for too long, but agrees that there is merit in incorporating training into a re-entry position in return for a decreased salary.

So, take the training position now, and who knows? You just might end up on the road with the Rolling Stones later.

## Don't Go Back Too Soon

There are some whose stories show that it is never too late to relaunch a legal career. Take Jim Addams, who relaunched his career after 25 years away from the practice of law. After graduating from Georgetown University Law Center in 1977, Addams began practicing law as an associate in the former firm of Brobeck Phleger & Harrison in San Francisco.

In 1982, Addams became an in-house counsel for Vulcan Materials Co. and accepted a management position in the company in 1986. He was chief operating officer of Holcim (US) Inc., the second-largest cement producer in the United States, until he retired in 2011.

Then on March 5, 2013, it was announced that Addams had joined the business and entertainment firm Shackelford, Melton & McKinley in Dallas as Of Counsel. His preparation for re-entry including taking bar exams and a bar review course, as to which Addams reported: "Of course, I was the grandfather in the classes."[6] In the hiring announcement, Addams was quoted as saying: "I don't think you ever stop being a lawyer . . . . Once a lawyer, always a lawyer."[7]

Susan Taylorson, a real estate firm associate, laughed when I asked about her "hiatus" from the law. "Hiatus? I guess you could call it that. I was gone for about 25 years." After leaving her banking practice in 1988 to be a full-time caregiver, including for her learning-disabled son, Taylorson says she loved every minute of being home. But when she turned 65, she decided it was "now or never" to go back to practicing. She enrolled in New Directions for Attorneys at Pace Law School, and ultimately started working for a small real estate firm after graduating from the program. A big departure from her previous experience? Maybe, she concedes. But then again, it was exactly the right fit for a woman who had, during her "hiatus," spent substantial time on the board of a co-op and managing properties in both England and New York City. When she did her externship with the New Directions program, she landed in the real estate finance bureau of the New York Attorney General's office, and found a true mentor in the department. A transition to real estate law became a logical next step for Taylorson.

Any regrets?

"I'm sorry I didn't get back a little sooner." Then again, she says that when she sees younger women balancing the demands of what she concedes is now a high-pressure job with their responsibilities at home, Taylorson says she knows she could not have come back to work too much sooner.

Caroll Welch was a commercial litigator for almost seven years at Winthrop before stepping away from the law for seven years. While she admits she missed it, she also says that during that time, "I completely separated from my identity as a lawyer." And when her youngest enrolled in school full-time, she "started to get the itch" to come back.

She was not interested in returning to the corporate law culture, and kept asking herself whether it was indeed the "right time." I asked Welch, "How do you know if it's the right time?"

Welch suggests that if you have a choice, and if you have a supportive spouse, partner, or network at home, those are key factors. Also, when you have exhausted the volunteer opportunities in your community and you feel the need for additional enrichment, it is a good time to consider going back. Welch had been active on the board of trustees for the library and the kids' schools, but after about seven years, she felt it was time to seek other opportunities.

Welch credits the New Directions for Attorneys program with allowing her to consider whether it was indeed the right time to come back to work. She says her unpaid externship obtained through the program allowed her to prepare her family for the idea of her working outside the home again. "It allowed everyone to see that now when they forget their trumpet at home, I probably can't go back and get it for them."

Solo practitioner Kim Yonta agrees that it is important to go back at the right time and on your own terms. After working as an assistant prosecutor in New Jersey for more than a decade, Yonta took less than two years off to be a full-time caregiver to her two children. When she started her own firm, she says she transitioned "slowly." She took on only part-time work and forged her own schedule around her personal obligations and the kids' school/extracurricular activities, until she was ready—in 2013—to make the solo law firm practice a full-time endeavor. As she navigated the transition back to full-time practice, Yonta said it was a "much easier process" than it would have been had she jumped back in too soon.

## It's the Technology (That Makes You Feel) Stupid

When I left the law, I was still keeping track of billables in my hardcover lawyer diary. Now there is an app and billing software that allows you to keep track of billable hours and matters. Small difference? Maybe.

But technology may be changing faster than the substantive law these days—which is a challenge of its own. Relaunching attorneys confirm—without exception—that they found getting up to speed on the technological changes in the office much more challenging than getting up to speed on the substantive legal issues.

Susan Taylorson, currently an associate at Gerstein Strauss & Rinaldi LLP, says that after 25 years away from the law, she had an easier time learning and familiarizing herself with the housing and real estate laws and regulations that are required knowledge in her new practice than adjusting to the technology advancements. She credits her getting up to speed on both to a wonderful mentor in the New York Attorney General's office. Taylorson also notes that she did not let her license lapse for too long—only a year or two—while she was away, and kept up on CLE classes, so that her transition back to practice was fairly smooth from that perspective.

Caren Ulrich Stacy, founder of OnRamp Fellowship, a program for relaunching attorneys, notes that technology can often be the biggest question mark for women re-entering the practice. She described one of the fellowship participants who, in her first week at work, was stymied when a partner asked her to "PDF something." The woman, she said, "didn't know if PDF was a noun or a verb. Fortunately, she Googled it and figured it out pretty quickly."[8]

Camille Raia, currently general counsel of Platinum Health Care, says that her decade away from the law starting in the mid-1990s was a crucial time in technology advancements. "Maybe if I had been away for some other 10-year period, it would not have been as big a deal. But those ten years were huge for technology."

Raia was a successful litigator in the 1980s and 1990s, opening a general practice firm in 1991 which her former husband eventually took over as Raia started having children. She says she always expected to go back to her practice "eventually," but when her marriage ended and her former practice dissolved, she was forced to think about going back earlier than planned. Like Susan Taylorson, Raia reports that she kept her license up and kept up with CLEs during her time away from the law, making that part of the transition easier.

OnRamp Fellowship's Caren Ulrich Stacy advises attorneys taking a break from the law to try to keep up to speed on technological advances the same way they keep up to date with substantive legal issues via CLE, coursework, and seminars. Enroll in PowerPoint seminars, look into classes at the local college or library. Keep fresh on legal skills, and keep even fresher on technology advances in the interim, no matter how long or short your "temporary" hiatus turns out to be.

Keep up with your self-assessment as well.

Also keep thinking about who you know.

## It's All About Who You Know

A few years ago, a friend of ours offered us killer seats to a major league baseball game. It was my then 7-year-old's first Major League baseball game and he brought along a glove to try to catch foul balls. I didn't have the heart to tell him the odds were not in his favor.

We were sitting in a section with lots of seasoned baseball fans, who were pretty aggressive every time a ball came even remotely close to us. My son started talking to the team's ball girl, who took an interest in this being his first time in this section—his first time at a Major League baseball game. He asked her questions about the players, and his genuine sincerity was apparently as evident to her as it was to me. When a foul ball came careening our way, my son was nearly trampled by the other would-be catchers armed with gloves and yells. The ball ricocheted off the wall near the piled-up fans and landed near the ball girl. An army of eager hands reached out for the ball, grabbing and clutching, but she put it in the stillest hand: that of a little boy with his eyes closed hopefully and his glove outstretched optimistically.

Just like with foul balls, in relaunching your career it's all about who you know.

Depending on how long you've been away from the profession, you may or may not know that the days of cold-calling employers and sending out blind résumés are gone. Save your stamps. Save your creamy, textured, résumé-grade bond paper.

That is not how you are going to get your next job.

You are going to get your next gig because of an externship you seek out, or from a contact of someone you meet at a networking event or a cocktail party, or while showing dogs as a hobby.

No, really.

Debra Vey Voda-Hamilton spent 13 years as a litigator and then 13 years away from the profession. "Thirteen seems to be my lucky number," she joked when we spoke in the summer of 2014. Voda-Hamilton spent her years away from the practice of law fundraising for and helping to run three different PTAs in three schools, in two different states, and pursuing her hobby of showing dogs. In 2008, with the collapse of the banking industry, since she had a banker husband, Voda-Hamilton decided it was time to dust off her law degree and return to the workforce.

She graduated from the New Directions for Attorneys program in 2009, and interviewed for 17 externship positions, believing that the experience of interviewing again was just as important as the practical experience she would gain through the program. She received 10 offers, and took a position preparing corporate documents with The Harlem Stage—one of the nation's leading arts organizations devoted to the creation and development of new works by performing artists of color. She even wrote to a former interviewer, someone who had offered a position she didn't take. "I apologized again for not taking the position, and then I asked to borrow some outlines on preparing corporate documents for my new position with The Harlem Stage." Which he sent.

After Voda-Hamilton graduated from the New Directions program (headed up by Amy Gewirtz), she decided to hang out her own shingle. She readily admits that her personal network from the 13 years away from the practice, including friends made through her hobby of showing dogs, created a pipeline of a variety of cases, including a seminal victory for an animal owner that garnered the attention of local print and TV press and led to Voda-Hamilton starting a business focused on mediation for cases involving animal conflicts.

Voda-Hamilton continues to network for her mediation business through speaking engagements. So much so that, as of the summer of 2014, she admits that her speaking career is the more lucrative and more time-consuming portion of her professional model. However, because she is such an advocate of mediation (indeed, she refuses to even take on any litigation cases, for fear of diluting her message), she hopes that will not always be the case.

She was a speaker at the 2013 American Veterinary Medical Law Association, discussing how employing alternative dispute resolution methodology in animal law conflicts may expedite resolution of veterinary malpractice and other client conflicts without the need for litigation. She has spoken at veterinary schools and conferences, the American Kennel Club, Human Animal Bond Organization, state bar association animal law committees, and animal interest groups outlining the value of using alternative dispute resolution in solving their own conflicts.

Erin Giglia, co-founder of Montage Legal Group, echoed the "it's all about who you know" message in a unique way when she freely conceded that part of the success of the fledgling company she co-founded with Laurie Rowen is "luck." "You never know when an opportunity is going to arise. You never know who you are talking to."

Casey Berman's roles as alternative legal career speaker and consultant really began as the result of his keeping in touch with his law school career office—which in 1999 invited him to speak to an audience whose engagement with his speech (many stayed to talk long after the scheduled speech had ended) proved to Casey a need for the consulting services he is now providing.

Carol Cohen agrees that it's who you know, and the ground-breaking book she co-authored, *Back on the Career Track*, gives some great advice about networking—the right way. "Nobody likes to feel used. You never want someone to think, 'She's just talking to me because I know so-and-so or because I work at _____ company.' If that is the only reason you're approaching someone, you have no right to do so. You've got to develop and show some interest in other people's lives and problems to be an effective networker."[9]

This is especially good advice for lawyers. As Montage Legal Group's Erin Giglia says, when you leave the law, you need to "re-learn how to connect" with friends and family. You may not be ready to network until you have truly relearned that skill. Start with the networks you already have (including those in your "just say yes" circles), before you start trying to connect in ways that might be perceived as artificial, forced, or contrived. Jill Backer, assistant dean for career and professional development at Pace University School of Law, points out that for transitioning attorneys, it may well be that the local bar association and committees provide the most robust networking opportunities.

In fact, Reid Hoffman, the co-founder of one of the best-known networking sites, LinkedIn, has said that you actually need two types of networks to succeed: acquaintances and allies.[10] Allies, according to Hoffman, are those contacts who are similar to you in personal and professional interests. These are not people you know only superficially. This type of network takes years to build.

In contrast to allies, acquaintances is a much bigger group (think Facebook "friend" list). This is your diverse group of contacts who are not necessarily directly in line with your professional and personal interests, although you may share things in common with them. These are the contacts that Hoffman says a site like LinkedIn can help amplify.[11] These are the contacts that might very well know someone who can help you relaunch your career, once you "say it out loud" to them. Of course, you have to have these contacts in your arsenal already; thus, it's important to create this network naturally and organically so that it's one you can actually tap into with sincerity when the time comes.

## Know Who You Are

Experts agree that continuous self-assessment is key to the transitioning process, and it is key to the relaunching process as well. Amy Gewirtz reports that the participants in the New Directions for Attorneys program fill out a self-assessment at the beginning of the program and seal it. Then, five months later, at the certificate award ceremony, they reopen it to see if anything has changed.

Self-assessment is not at all passive; it is an active process. You should continue to keep skills fresh—through technology courses, CLE courses, even by advocating for something you feel passionate about. Consider *pro bono* work. Keep up bar association memberships, and follow and/or join interesting committees. Continue to network and keep in touch with career counseling offices of your alma mater(s). Keep up a LinkedIn profile. Make a business card and carry it with your title "attorney at law," along with relevant contact information. Join alumni groups, and think about your elevator speech—that is, what you want to "say out loud."

Do all of these things to "keep your foot in the door of the profession," says Gewirtz. They are all means and avenues of self-analysis as you continue your post-transition journey.

As part of the continuing self-assessment and critical analysis needed to re-enter the legal profession, you are going to need to recognize the professional skills you've learned during your time away from the profession, but embrace the skills learned in the profession and in your legal training as well. Gretchen Rubin is a *New York Times* best-selling author and lawyer-turned-happiness-expert. Says Rubin: "'Know thyself.' It's one of the biggest lessons I learned during the Happiness Project. It's the oldest advice in the world—to know thyself. What can be more vital than that?"[12]

In fact, without exception, every transitioning lawyer I interviewed for this book—including international Lego brick artist Nathan Sawaya, who concedes that he never really wanted to be a lawyer and rarely acknowledges himself as a lawyer these days—offered that the skills they gained during law school and practicing law proved to be a differentiator in their post-law-firm lives. The same can be true for relaunchers.

Once a lawyer, always a lawyer.

If you want to be.

Or even if you don't want to be.

Put simply, being a lawyer—or having *been* a lawyer—can help you in many ways, including being one *again*.

So remember to constantly assess *who* you are. It's an inquiry that is likely to have nothing at all to do with the fact that you are a lawyer.

And probably always will be one.

## Notes

1. Carol Cohen & Vivian Rabin, *Back on the Career Track: A Guide for Stay-at-Home-Moms Who Want to Return to Work* (Hachette Book Group USA, 2007), at 7.

2. http://ms-jd.org/blog/article/beeatitudes-keep-not-settling.

3. Carol Cohen & Vivian Rabin, *Back on the Career Track: A Guide for Stay-at-Home-Moms Who Want to Return to Work* (Hachette Book Group USA, 2007), at 179.

4. http://onrampfellowship.com/.

5. *Id.*

6. http://texaslawyer.typepad.com/texas_lawyer_blog/2013/03/newsmakers-lawyer-returns-to-practicing-law-after-more-than-25-year-break.html.

7. *Id.*

8. Ellen Rosen, *Firms Hiring Women Returning to Practice: Business of Law*, Bloomberg Businessweek (September 25, 2014), http://www.businessweek.com/news/2014-09-25/firms-hiring-women-returning-to-practice-business-of-law.

9. Carol Cohen & Vivian Rabin, *Back on the Career Track: A Guide for Stay-at-Home-Moms Who Want to Return to Work* (Hachette Book Group USA, 2007), at 5.

10. Mika Salmi & Reid Hoffman, *You Need Two Types of Professional Networks*, LinkedIn (July 16, 2013), https://www.linkedin.com/pulse/article/20130716185520-45185363-reid-hoffman-you-need-two-types-of-professional-networks.

11. *Id.*

12. Ashby Jones, *On Happiness and Lawyers: A Chat with Gretchen Rubin, Part II*, Wall St. J. Law Blog (September 24, 2009), http://blogs.wsj.com/law/2009/09/24/on-happiness-and-lawyers-a-chat-with-gretchen-rubin-part-ii/.

# Appendix

# Additional Resources for
# Interrupted Lawyers

- ABA Directory of State Bar Programs for Lawyers in Transition: http://www.americanbar.org/groups/leadership/office_of_the_president /legal_access_jobs_corps/lajc_resource_center/programs_for_lawyers _in_transition.html
- A Better Balance: http://www.abetterbalance.org/web
- Above the Law: Career Alternatives: http://abovethelaw.com/ career-alternatives
- American University Washington College of Law Lawyer Re-Entry Program
  Office of Academic Affairs
  4801 Massachusetts Avenue, NW, Suite 362
  Washington, DC 20016
  Email: lawyer.reentry@wcl.american.edu
  Phone: 202-274-4138
  http://www.wcl.american.edu/reentry/
- Bliss Lawyers: Deborah Henry Epstein, Suzie Scanlon Rabinowitz, & Garry Berger, *Finding Bliss: Innovative Legal Models for Happy Clients & Happy Lawyers* (ABA Publishing, 2015), http://www.blisslawyers .com
- But I Do Have a Law Degree: http://www.butidohavealawdegree.com
- Gretchen Rubin: My Experiments in the Pursuit of Happiness and Good Habits: http://www.gretchenrubin.com/

- iRelaunch: Carol Fishman Cohen & Vivian Steir Rabin, *Back on the Career Track: A Guide for Stay-at-Home Moms Who Want to Return to Work* (Hachette Book Group USA, 2007), http://www.irelaunch.com
- JAMS Arbitration, Mediation, and ADR Services: http://www.jamsadr.com
- JD Careers Out There: http://jdcareersoutthere.com
- Lawyer Career Spa: http://lawyercareerspa.com
- Lawyer's Guide to Networking: Susan Schneider, *A Lawyers Guide to Networking* (ABA Publishing, 2006)
- *Life After Law:* Liz Brown, *Life After Law: Finding Work You Love with the J.D. You Have* (Bibliomotion, 2013), http://lizbrownjd.com
- Leave Law Behind: http://leavelawbehind.com
- Mother Attorneys Mentoring Association (MAMA): http://www.mamaseattle.org
- Montage Legal Group: http://montagelegal.com
- New Directions for Attorneys, Pace Law School
  78 North Broadway
  White Plains, New York 10603
  (914) 422-4606
  http://www.law.pace.edu/newdirections
- The New Perfect: Beaupre Gillespie & Hollee Temple, *Good Enough Is the New Perfect: Finding Success and Happiness in Modern Motherhood* (Harlequin Nonfiction, 2011), http://thenewperfect.com
- On-Ramp Fellowship Program: http://onrampfellowship.com
- The Other Bar: Supporting Recovery in the Legal Community: http://www.otherbar.org/
- Solo Practice University: http://solopracticeuniversity.com

# Acknowledgments

Thank you to ABA Publishing for enthusiastically green-lighting this book, and to Rick Paszkiet, Marisa L'Heureux, and Kathy Welton for championing the project from beginning to end.

I often say that I loved being a practicing lawyer until I didn't. That I loved it so much—and for so long—is a testament to the wonderful professional mentors and colleagues I had along the journey. And while there were far too many to list by name, there were several people/groups along the way that I consider "landmarks" along my professional journey and I would be remiss if I did not mention the following by name and give thanks:

- To the Honorable Gary Golkiewicz, my first "boss" as a new lawyer, who taught me more about fairness, the pragmatic administration of justice, and the need to write clearly *even* when writing about the law than any who came before or after
- To Mark Landman, mentor and founding partner of the firm where I spent some of my favorite years as a litigator: Landman, Corsi, Ballaine & Ford P.C.
- To my first associate colleagues in the Newark office of Landman, Corsi, Ballaine & Ford, especially my comrade Eleanor Armstrong, with whom I learned that the practice of law would always require equal parts of hard work, a steel backbone, and caffeine
- To my dear friend Paula Tziavragos, to whom I had the great honor of being assigned as a "mentor" when she first began her legal career, and who ultimately became a great mentor and inspiration to *me*—both in her journey to partnership, and later as an "interrupted" lawyer like myself
- To the entire current and past Mass Torts Department at Skadden Arps, whom I had the miraculous pleasure of learning from and working with during the most fascinating decade of my legal career

Thank you to all of the transitioning attorneys—both named and unnamed in this book—who contributed invaluably with their anecdotes, their inspiration, and their courage.

So, so, so much gratitude to my husband, Paul, who suffered in silence (a remarkable feat if you know him!) as I neglected him (and so many things!) to make my deadlines for this book, and for saying, on the eve of my final deadline, what felt like the single most romantic thing anyone has ever said in the history of time: "How about if I stay up with you tonight and help you proofread?" *Swoon.*

And of course, to my children: Paul, Luke, and Grace. They often brag that I left the practice of law to "be home with" them. But the truth is, I left the law neither to be "home" nor "with" them. I left the practice of law to be many places—but in all of those places—to be *for them.*

# Index